ARTISTS: A KANSAS COLLECTION

TEXT: PATRIC ROWLEY — PHOTOGRAPHY: STEVE HARPER

DEDICATION

JANET CURTIS COREY DUNHAM

On her last trip to Castine, Maine, in the fall of 1985, Mother spent much of her time looking out the window at the blooming flowers against the dark wooded background on one side and the deep blue of the harbor on the right.

She was seeing her garden where the variety of textures and riot of color gave her reason to smile. Her life was like that of a gardener, sowing seeds of love and encouragement to "be all that we could possibly be and to do all that we could possibly do and then celebrate with great joy."

In her garden, we are sure that if the cricket were quiet, we could hear the ant sing. Harmony is there as it has been in creating this book. We, too, can smile and most certainly celebrate!

—Barbara Corey Mallonee

ARTISTS: A KANSAS COLLECTION

Published in 1989 by Artists Registry, Inc.
Wichita, Kansas.

Text: Patric Rowley — Photography: Steve Harper
Editors: Betty Rowley and Barbara Mallonee

Library of Congress Catalog Card Number: 89-84476
ISBN 0-9623079-0-4

First Edition
Printed and bound in the United States of America

Acknowledgments

Book design, typography and production art:
Patric Rowley & Partners—Betty Rowley, Janice Simpson, Jim Simpson and Christopher Whittington

Cover design: Barbara Mallonee
Slide selection: Jane Eby and Reuben Saunders

Assistant editing: Charles Pearson and Barbara Rowley

Typographic output: The Typesetter, Inc.—Doris Anton

Proofing: Alta Brock, Anne Clevenger and Helen Ferrell

Printing: McCormick-Armstrong Company, Inc.
Pete Armstrong

Printed on 100# Vintage Gloss and 80# Mountie Gloss
Potlatch Corp., N.W. Paper Division from
Southwest Paper Company—John Tangeman

Transparencies: Chromatech—Ron Wilson

Color separations and duotones: Edwards Typographic Service, Inc.—Waldo Leisy

Elite photographic paper provided by Kodak

The Artists Registry, Inc., emerged in January of 1984 as a not-for-profit corporation from a small gallery started by Barbara Mallonee in 1981. This original operation provided visual artists in residence, art enthusiasts and collectors one location in which to find each other through exhibitions and a library of slides of artwork and information.

The long-term goal of the Artists Registry is to create a library of information about artists, both present and past, who have lived and worked in Kansas; to find new and unusual sources of exhibition space; to educate our school children about the creative opportunities and importance of art in our everyday existence; to encourage sales of artwork for public as well as private enjoyment; and to share information through the publication of fine quality books.

Acknowledgments

Any project of this magnitude, and in this case, an unprecedented book, cannot be done without a lot of help. For this, I want to express much gratitude to each staunch member of the Executive Board of the Artists Registry, Inc.: Ralph Brock, Jon Callen, Christine Christy, Scott McMillan and Reuben Saunders. A special brand of talent, humor and support was needed to carry the completion of this book to the finish line. They supplied that reinforcement.

The book project has given me a reason to remember the many friends and new faces who supported the concept of a showcase for artists of the heartland.

From that first trip to New York to test the concept—when Gordon Parks and Steve Rooney, Director of the Administration of the International Center of Photography, affirmed the idea, the book became a goal. In Washington, D.C., Wilhelmina Holladay, who was in the process of founding the National Museum of Women in the Arts, was a fountainhead of encouragement. All agreed that there definitely is an interest in the culture springing from these grass roots. There just isn't a budget to explore it. However, a book is portable. And a book seemed possible.

The juried competition to select the artists to be featured was a joint effort with the Kansas Arts Commission and the five judges were: Reuben Saunders, Wichita; Ann Evans, Lawrence; John Thorns, Jr., Hays; Gayle Davis, Wichita; and Paul Beauchamp, Topeka. Dodge Thompson of the Smithsonian Institute, Washington, D.C., endorsed the finalists and we were underway.

I am grateful for those friends who served on the Board during these years: Peter Beren, Kelly Callen, Betty Dillon, Lucinda Foster, Gary Fugit, Jean Garvey, Shirley Glickman, Martha Healy, Millie Hill, Richard Minkler and Tom Tracy. And the organizational and fundraising skills of Robin Bair, Gifford Booth, Gingy Buck, Jan Deering and Barbara Ritchie were essential to our survival.

It was the generosity of the companies involved in the production and the encouragement (fortified with funds) from the friends who responded, that allowed us to go to press. Thank you one and all!

—BARBARA MALLONEE

ARTISTS: A KANSAS COLLECTION

This book was made possible by generous contributions for which the Artists Registry, Inc. is most grateful.

FOUNDERS

The Charitable Foundation, Inc.
George and Jacqueline Charno
Christine Christy
Ace and Betty Dillon
Dick and Carolyn Dillon
Janet C. Corey Dunham
Wayne Kirkman
The Fred C. Koch Foundation, Inc.
Mary Koch
Price R. and Flora A. Reid Foundation
Ritchie Foundation, Inc.
Paul Ross Charitable Foundation

PATRONS

Bank IV Wichita
Peter Beren
S.O. Beren Foundation
Misco Charitable Trust
Ralph and Alta Brock
The Coleman Charitable Trust, Inc.
Jack and Marilyn DeBoer
Janet Curtis Corey Dunham Memorial
Edwards Typographic Service, Inc.
Gary Fugit
Garvey Kansas Foundation
Kansas Arts Commission
Senator Nancy Kassebaum
David and Janet Murfin
The Wichita Eagle-Beacon

BENEFACTORS

Mark and Helen Adams
Joan Beren
Bob and Gingy Buck
Jon and Kelly Callen
Eugene G. Coombs and Family
Chain and Martha Healy
Kansas Gas and Electric Company
Scott McMillan
Richard and Betty Minkler
Reuben and Vonda Saunders
Stan Wisdom

FRIENDS

Thornton Anderson
Mary Sally Aylward
John Bell
Harold and Boots Bergman
David Bernard
Mrs. Merie Davis Bish
Jim and Mary Boyd
Charlotte Brickler
Ron Christ and Barbara Mason
Helen Dorman
Emprise Bank
Ben and Lucinda Foster
Fink Foundation
Friends of the Wichita Art Museum
Olive W. Garvey
Garvey Foundation
Willard and Jean Garvey
Pat Gillespie
Milton and Gladys Glickman
William and Shirley Glickman
Mr. and Mrs. H. D. Hale
Royce Harper
Robert and Jo Harris
Jack and Lenora Heathman
M. Meredith Hill
Wilhelmina Cole Holladay
Jan Seymour Jenkins
Louis and Rhonda Johnson
Kansas Gas and Electric Company
John and Mickey Leiter
Mrs. Frank Malone
Mildred J. Marcus
R.D. and Eleanor Martens
Dr. and Mrs. George Mastio
Nancy Means
Dr. Jim and Betty Menehan
Hamilton and Betty Mitchell
Bill and Betty Murfin
Fred and Moira Lee Murfin
Mr. and Mrs. John Naftzger
Jeff and Diane Newton
Clyde and Marty Nichols
Minnie Phipps Estate
Helen W. Piper
Joan Prater
Ray Reed
Jim Reeder
Proctor and Vivian Ritchie
Don Schrag
Clifford Stone
Bill and Georgia Teich
Merle Davis Ties
Whimsey, Inc.
C. Howard Wilkins
Milo and Mame Wright
Jeanne Yankey

DONORS

Mrs. Frances C. Aitchison
Anita Allison
Harlan and Ginny Altman
Robert S. and Joan L. Bader
Jim and Carolyn Beckett
Fred and Sally Bell
Philomene Bennett and Louis Marak
Anne Marie Bercik
Rita Blitt
Gifford and Natalie Booth
Virginia Bowden
Howard and Helen Boys
Carolyn Bradley
Dr. Frank and Betty Brosius
John and Mary Brown
Duane and Janet Buckley
Mr. and Mrs. John Burns
Francis and Saddy Carr
Santo Catanese
Don and Kathy Coons
Mrs. Ben W. Curtis, Sr.
John and Ruth Coultis
Lucille Corey
Robert and Ruth Corey
Ed and Olene Curtis
Joyce and Ridgley Denning
Tom and Myra Devlin
Gus and Dottie di Zerega
A. Joseph Everson
Mrs. Doyle Fair
Helen Ferrell
Jay and Helen Galloway
Nancy Garretson
Leonard and Ivonne Goldstein
Dr. Hew and Judy Goodpasture
Tom Gormally
David and Marilyn Grisham
Peg Hale
Dean Ashmore Harris
Mr. and Mrs. Thomas E. Harrison, Jr.
Boots and Ken Hartstein
Lee Anne Hays
Frank E. and Harriet E. Hedrick Foundation
Norma Hewitt
Jo Hiebert
Mr. and Mrs. Ken Johnson
Peter and Marilyn Johnson
Shirley Joseph
Emily Kelly
Ted and Marjorie Kendall
John and Jeanette Kennaday
Bob and Barbara Kiskadden
George and Margo Kren
Fred and Chris Kubik
Tom and Nan Lahey
Dorothy Langenwalter
Harry Litwin
Elizabeth Mallonee
Marvin and Eleanor Martin
Zelma Napier
Bob and Martha Oestreicher
Jim and Carol Olander
Innes and Patsy Phillips
Georgia Ptacek
Dean and Barbara Ritchie
Polly Rombold
Stephen Schuetz
Mrs. William Stanley Skaer
Pat Gaines Talbott
Dr. Harvey and Julie Tretbar
Byrne and Becky Vickers
Wichita State Bank
Ruth M. Winsor
Mrs. Frank Wiswall
Mary Wurth
Oleta Yost

K
KANSAS ARTS COMMISSION

ARTISTS: A KANSAS COLLECTION

ARTISTS: A KANSAS COLLECTION, Continued

Introduction

It seems like I've been looking at pictures forever. In my mind's eye I can see a great river of images, stretching out on either bank to my peripheral limits and disappearing downstream over the dark edges of my memory. Even though they were collected with no purpose and arranged in no special order, I can reach back and retrieve any one of countless pictures from my cluttered gallery.

I remember labels from canned goods that I collected for a third grade project. I don't recall the real purpose of the assignment, but at this moment, more than a half century later, I can instantly recreate the vividly tantalizing look of the Del Monte peach label, carefully trimmed and pasted down on a sheet of Big Chief tablet paper.

At that moment, I learned to recognize a masterpiece. It's not a thing, I learned, as much as it is a time—the instant at which beauty and the beholder reach a level of intimacy that creates something akin to an out-of-body experience. For a split second, we see the essence of ourselves through the abstraction of beauty. It's a sort of purifying experience, a nice feeling that is open to all who are open to it.

Pictures, visual images of any kind on any subject dominate my life. Nature first, then art. Then movies and television and magazines and picture books and billboards. And product labels and T-shirts. And the comics. I gulp them down like a thirsty desert rat. Even after all these years, I hate to keep my eyes closed long enough to get an average good night's sleep.

Among my treasures is the sight of blooming wild strawberries in an Oklahoma-red ditch; an orange Volkswagen putting across a cobalt blue horizon; a city park full of ice-encased trees in silver-grey moonlight; yellow leaves rolling down freshly asphalted streets; a huge rock used as a signboard for the religious admonition to repent. The rich black, brown and rust streaks from a leaky faucet on the white cement wall of a rural store near Fairland, Oklahoma. And the strange Indian drawings on a canyon wall somewhere in southern Utah. I remember them all—and I guess I always will.

When I'm not seeing pictures or thinking about them or putting

them into my own drawings and paintings, I talk about them. Once in Panama, I saw this man walking along very nonchalantly in a heavy tropical rain while a woman walked behind sheltering him with a huge banana leaf. He seemed to be in deep thought, leaving little clouds of cigar smoke in his wake. The woman wore a simple dress and a head scarf and she was soaked to the skin. All around them was a jungle so intensely green that you couldn't see any other color.

When I was in my thirties, several men about my age and their sons joined my son and me for an overnight stay in a rancher's cabin deep in the Flint Hills. I got up before sunrise and walked away from the cabin and sat on a ridge to watch the night end and the day begin. What I saw was a smooth-edged, perfectly round red-orange sun, hanging over dark green and black folds in the pasture. Then a coyote trotted to a position where he became silhouetted against the sun and stood there for a few seconds. And then it all vanished. Except what I remember.

A good part of seeing is the kind that filters out through the creative imagination, adding to what has been seen by the eyes only. That's how a child can make a monster out of a night shadow. And that's how artists are able to show us things the way we could never see them without their help. Save only a few, the really special seeing experiences of my life have been paintings, prints and drawings and other kinds of art. I have found that even the most spectacular sights like the moon filling the sky over the Caribbean can gain new dimensions through the artist's eye and hand and creative courage.

I still have this deep-down craving to see all the art I can see. After all these years of visiting museums, galleries and artists' studios, my step still quickens as I go to visit yet another place where I can feast on artist's visions. Who knows what there is around the corner?

This book was a special joy for me because it gave me an opportunity to see the amazingly diverse works of 44 artists who were selected by jury to provide the inaugural show for the new National Museum of Women in the Arts in Washington, D.C.

Some of what I saw, you can see. Some of what I learned about them, you can know. That's what this book is about. And even though it isn't as good as being there, it should give you at least an idea of what's out there.

—PATRIC ROWLEY

Photographer's Comments

When I was asked to participate in the making of this book, I figured the challenge of photographing over 40 artists was something I couldn't pass up. Experience has taught me that making a portrait of anyone is a difficult proposition, and since I have had the good fortune of being around artists most of my life, I knew this would be the ultimate challenge in visual soul gathering.

Artists are by their nature enigmas wrapped in a mystery and although this project involved several years, I would have no more than a couple hours with each subject, some much less. Add to that the fact that almost none of these folks knew me from Adam—and you have a truly interesting task. And so it went. Appointments were made, equipment gathered and off I went to Kansas City, Wellsville, Lawrence, Emporia, Hays, El Dorado, Manhattan and, of course, Wichita.

Most everyone was patient, friendly and in some cases, rather camera shy. Some were like myself and enjoyed a good chat about almost anything, while others gave me the time necessary to make their picture—but had little time for anything else.

I enjoyed this visual odyssey and logged some enjoyable miles in my old VW bug. There is no wasted time on the road as long as you look around—and I look around a lot. I made some pretty fair Kansas landscape shots while traveling to or from my appointed rounds so I got more out of this than the pleasure of meeting new people.

If I have failed to capture the total essence of each artist, I hope I have at least touched on a facet of their personality. The individuals on these pages were the challenge I thought they would be, and for that I am grateful. The world would be a sad and dull place without the vision of artists and we are doubly blessed to have so many of them living in Kansas, the heart and soul of the "Great Plains."

—STEVE HARPER

JANE ASBURY The soft, cultivated voice of Jane Asbury is slightly accented with a broad "A." Her manners are gracious and correct. She serves tea with the proper amount of ceremony. She is a small woman with a handsome face and bright, inquisitive eyes. Nothing seems to escape her. The most subtle nuances of what is said or implied seem instantly to be a part of her thoughts and her responses. And it's all accomplished easily and naturally in harmony with the ebb and flow of conversation.

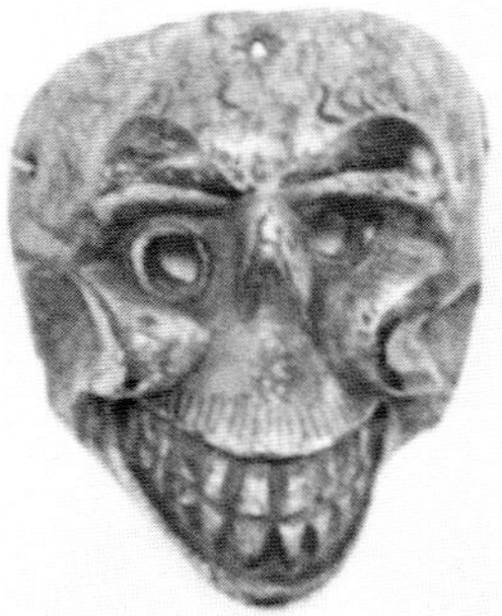

There is no stress, no sense of coiled-up aggressive energy, impatient to strike. What you get is a thoughtful, well-conceived and quietly articulated answer. Yet there is also some of the savant, the sorcerer, the magician in Jane Asbury. She practices the art of the illusionist. She can describe things in an unfamiliar language in ways that make the unexplainable more understandable. What she is drawn to is the magic of what happens when she creates her images, she explained.

Making her art is a very personal process. Only a small part of it is analytical. What she paints is mined from her subconscious, memories of desert rocks and minerals that go all the way back to her childhood.

Jane Asbury grew up a short walk from the Museum of Natural History in New York City. Both of her parents were artists and there was a studio at home. Even in mid-town Manhattan, nature was an important part of her experience. The great forests of trees and shrubs and grass-covered fields of Central Park were along her ordinary pathways, and she spent hours in the Natural History Museum. There were art lessons, concerts, museum trips and other opportunities to learn and to grow.

Today she is far away from her roots, engaged in bold inquiries into a very large, very complex body of subject material. The widening center of her curiosity is the nature of change in the world. What began as a child's fascination with the strange shapes and colors and textures of carefully catalogued mineral exhibits in a New York City museum have expanded into personal expeditions into the American Southwest in search of clues that can be used in paintings to interpret her thoughts on transformation and change. Her work has led to two University of Kansas Research Grants: "Painting Series on Elemental Transformations in Landscape" and "Painting Series Exploring Sand As a Medium."

For five years she has roamed the mountains and deserts of the Southwest, exploring stone formations and mineral deposits and studying pictographs and petroglyphs left behind by ancient Indian cultures. The mountains, ravines and canyon walls and the huge, eroding rocks speak to her in very special ways. She senses the implications of the earth as a continuous moving and transitional organism. And to her it becomes what it has been for many years: a recurring theme of personal life changes flowing into the larger pattern of changes in nature. The result creates more questions than answers, but the subject is one that must be addressed. It is, after all, how she sees the world, and to be in harmony with the perpetual state of change of the earth, she acknowledges her need to question and to re-examine.

As an accomplished painter, printmaker, sculptor and art historian, she is well equipped to deal with the work she has chosen to do. Even though the idiom appears to be strongly influenced by abstract expressionism, it incorporates other sources from American Indian to African; from Klee to Tomayo. Behind it all, there is a warm primal sense of the earth's history, a kind of unpeeling process at work in the selection of color, texture and form.

The paintings she makes are mysterious, enigmatic statements of swirling, twisting shapes, floating in space. The shape-inventions and their placement are intuitional. There are no rules governing what they are, what they are doing, or why. They are simply what they are. And what they are is up to everyone who sees them.

Navajo Song. Oil on canvas, 49½″ x 35¾″

The mountains, ravines and canyon walls and the huge, eroding rocks speak to her in very special ways.

Philomene Bennett I wish I had been lucky enough to have had Philomene Bennett as a big sister when I was growing up. She is beautiful and warm and wise. She can look at you and make you feel important and cared for. And all of this wonderful warmth and wit seems tightly interwoven into her art.

Under her hand, complex fiberglass constructions glitter and twist their way into smaller, simpler, more basic emotional meanings. Slathers of heavy pigment and slashes of bold brash color suddenly convert into deeply mysterious, strangely familiar images. You see her art everywhere. Paintings. Sculpture. Ceramics. Prints. Drawings. She produces art like a natural spring produces pure water. And so does her husband.

Philomene and Lou Marak work together, live together and shape their lives out of the same substance. Together, they have a united family of nine children; four from her first marriage and five from his. Each has lost a child; a son of hers, a daughter of his. They stand together now as self-employed artists, quite easily the world's most uncertain profession.

What Philomene and her husband do requires massive self-confidence, limitless physical energy, boundless emotional resiliency and incredible good fortune. Most of whatever they do, they do on their own: paintings on mural size canvas, experimenting with drawings on great sheets of paper, making fiberglass and ceramic constructions.

To supplement their art sales income, Philomene teaches and Lou makes cartoons for greeting cards. Somehow both seem to have the capacity to make time for all the things they want to pursue.

They live on a farm only a quarter of a mile away from one of the countless cloverleaf ramps that take people on and off the expressways surrounding Kansas City. But their place seems long ago and far away, like something out of *Currier and Ives*. The buildings are nestled in a forest of enormous trees. Goats, chickens and guinea hens scamper about in the big barnyard. Clocks, calendars and deadlines would seem out of place and unnecessary in this remote place.

The interior of their house is like a very intimate, very comfortable live-in museum. All the rooms flow together like galleries and all the tables, chairs, sofas and furnishings are placed so that if you pause at a painting or print or drawing, there is a comfortable place right where you are to sit and look at it. In one room, a large sensuous abstract expressionist painting literally takes my breath away. With obvious pride, Philomene identifies it as one of Lou's.

Their cavernous studio, a huge converted barn, allows them the space to work as large as they wish, in whatever medium they choose. They stretch their own canvas, make frames, build crates to ship their work and fire ceramics in their own kiln.

In much of Philomene's work, content is more important than the medium. A large fiberglass totem is for her son, dead from an automobile accident at age 18. It is more than a passive memorial. There is a crimson heart floating in the entangled shapes and textures of the construction—a valentine for Michael.

A painting hanging on a wall near the totem seems to shout out a joyful hymn. Fragments of intense blues and oranges and white and black twist through a maze of heavily pigmented shapes to emerge as feelings of sun, mountains and water. It is called *Great Heaven Rock* and it could be anything, or everything.

Once, early in her career, a prolonged exposure to the minimalism then in vogue left her with an empty, resentful feeling. "My life isn't a nothing; it's full of excitement and joy and color and texture and line. The imagery will come out, whatever it is and wherever it comes from."

Instead of following the precepts of any school or line of thought, Philomene often starts painting and lets the painting lead her where it will. The result is work with its own kind of sophistication. It is not contrived; it is most certainly not a product of random accident. It has an enormous amount of emotional vitality, but there is a soothing sense of kindness and caring in what it suggests. It is easy to like, but challenging to know.

Layer Above, 1983. Acrylic on canvas, 60" x 66"

"My life isn't a nothing; it's full of excitement and joy and color and texture and line."

DAVID BERNARD I have known David since he arrived in Wichita shortly after World War II. As I walk the path to his door, I remember how he looked when I first saw him. He seems to be a little grayer, a little thinner, the creases on his face a little deeper. There is a piece of sculpture near the entrance to his house, a small limestone carving by one of his former students and colleagues, a single sign that this is an artist's household. I am amazed at how little David's youthful smile has changed and how persistently and spontaneously it appears.

There are several pieces of his sculpture visible from where we sit and a number of his intaglio prints are hung about the room. He shows me a book he has made called *Ten Mayan Gods*. Each subject in it is illustrated with an aquatint and page design linoleum cuts. It is a big book, printed on crisp paper. The typography, the binding, everything in the book is a work of art, a product of careful and deliberate choices, of long, sustained creative effort. There were only eleven books published, one of which is in the collection of the Library of Congress. It is typical of his work. The craftsmanship is tight and solid, the sort of neat and seamless look that shows no outward signs of toil or stress. And yet there is a very subtle primitive cast, a slight flattening out of the perspective, a deft editing of nonessential detail leaving a sort of bare innocence that speaks with a powerful and provocative voice.

The choice of subject matter doesn't seem to be of primary importance to him. He moves easily from intaglios of ancient Mayan temples to linocuts of nostalgic recollections of farm life. He uses black in a heavy, structural way, like Rouault. Brighter, lighter colors like alizarin crimson and cerulean blue seem to gain in intensity and clarity as they escape from the heavy black matrix.

There is also a quiet, scholarly undertone to his work, reflecting his background training and teaching experience in the history of art. Many of his early intaglios, he says, were conceived as commentaries on the problems of war, politics and decadence. He sometimes uses religious themes and has lately become fascinated by the relationship of humanity to the land or to the sea.

In all of David Bernard's life–his home, his work, his manner–there is a detached serenity that hovers like an aura of goodwill. After collecting hundreds of honors and achieving a rare level of respect and affection from his peers, he seems now to be thinking about the distant possibilities for a peaceful, harmonious world. Outwardly, he appears to be a straightforward, simple man; a man of deep commitment. "It is the mission of the artist," he believes, "to create order and structure. These things are permanent and through them the artist hopes to create visual poetry."

Mitla, 1985. Seven color woodcut, 18" x 24"

John Boyd The ink, watercolor and acrylic interpretation of John Boyd's Frankenstein's monster brought back old memories. I saw the film, *Frankenstein*, during its original release in the thirties. It was a dark and shadowy night late in autumn and I had gone to the theater alone. One of the more exciting parts of the film was the long pursuit of Dr. Frankenstein's creation by a large and unruly mob of villagers who carried flaming torches, shotguns and pitchforks. In spite of his size and strength, there was plainly a mismatch between monster and mob. By the climax of the film, he had become an object of my sympathy and I was sad to see him perish in the flames of the castle. I also was puzzled and feeling a little guilty about why I felt such melancholy for a monster made of spare parts.

John Boyd knows why. His parody, *The New Frankenstein*, is one of an eerie suite of six works which include Dracula, Wolfman, King Kong, The Mummy and Dr. Jeckyl and Mr. Hyde. He chose these creatures, he says, because of their significant social and philosophical meanings. Even though they were created to frighten us, Boyd believes they are also underdogs, and as such, they represent the ordinary people of our society who are also victims. We can, it seems, all identify with downtrodden monsters.

John Boyd is a funny fellow in a very special way. He doesn't tell jokes. He invents insanely, irrepressibly, joyously strange images that make you feel as if you don't know whether to laugh or cry. His brand of wit is used in the same context as that of other masters of parody in that he peels away disguises and reveals a sharper focus on reality. He uses his art, his wildly imaginative prints and paintings and drawings to do it.

They can be outrageously indifferent to conventional expectations. The peculiar frame on *The New Frankenstein* with its "Zap-Zam" inscription, for example, has no apparent purpose or rational meaning, but it belongs in a way that makes it completely indispensable. A comically fat ape wearing boxer shorts, hovering over the Empire State Building ineffectually swatting at attacking aircraft becomes a tragic figure in Boyd's color lithograph, *King Kong*. In all that John Boyd does, it seems that there is a sort of comic touch tinged with a long, low mournful note of contrition.

John Boyd's parodies come from anywhere. He has used historical images like Jan van Eyck's *Giovanni Arnolfini and His Bride* and Della Francesca's *The Duke of Urbino*. He has parodied the manners of Matisse and Duchamp. He has used Kafka and Blake and other literary sources for his parodies. In recent years, he has turned to his own life for subject material, a step which has allowed him to invent more freely and prodigiously than ever before. It was this

that led him to his monster series.

Beyond the messages, John Boyd is also a virtuoso of art and media. He paints and makes prints, carves and does paper casting in endless combinations and configurations. He has a sure touch, a practiced hand and a sharp eye.

When he was a child in Arkansas, he learned about self-sufficiency. He remembers that when his father needed a new hoe handle, he just found a straight hickory limb, cut it, skinned it, and shaped and sized it by hand. Rooms were built; fence posts cut; fruits and vegetables planted, harvested, canned and eaten all on the same piece of ground. He has a warm recollection of the quilting bees, the bright patches of cloth, the quick dancing fingers and the hum of conversation. Boyd collects small wood carvings and whistles and other folk art memorabilia. He borrows some of the same feeling for his own work. The central objects in his compositions emerge with a slightly awkward, primitive look, faintly reminiscent of comic books, school yard graffiti and folk art icons like painted wood carvings of Uncle Sam and cigar store Indians.

In his work, he tries to act out moralistic plays: good versus evil. The compositional format is like a stage setting. He chose the flat cartoon style of drawing because of his interest and admiration for Picasso, Magritte and the surrealists, and for the fact that it evokes a deep and mysterious mood, beyond ordinary terms of reality. "The pictures I make," he says, "are humorous, sad, satirical, witty and sometimes profound. I couldn't wish for anything more."

Portrait of Rembrandt, 1986. Paper cast and intaglio print, 12″ x 12″ x ½″

Vernon Brejcha The clicking sound comes from a small computer control changing the settings on an electric kiln. It's a necessary device if Vernon Brejcha is to afford to continue glassblowing. The cost of gas and electricity can run into hundred of dollars and the expense of other materials such as powdered minerals and dyes can totally demolish the budget of a professor of art.

Some way, the thing has to be self-supporting. There are, however, many obstacles to overcome. While glass was used to create art during the Renaissance in Venice, it has recovered whatever status it had as an art form only since the mid-point of this century. And even though glass art has become popular with some, it is still not a big seller in Kansas. Or, for that matter, throughout most of the nation. And finally, it has to be recognized that for all of its resistance to fading or discoloration or other hazards of aging, the time, energy, money and artistic inspiration invested in glass can be lost in less than a second if it is mishandled or if fate decrees an entirely unmerited accident.

These thoughts must sometimes occur to Vernon Brejcha but the idea of giving it up is a thoroughly unacceptable option. As one of the disciples involved in the resurgence of glass as an art medium, he has tasted its sweet and heady wine and only glass, he will tell you, can express and enhance the artist's vision of fluidity with the same degree of completeness.

The refraction, reflection and polish of glass are important but nothing, absolutely nothing, is more relevant than the fact that it provides the means to create a small, clear world inside walls of glass. No matter what the frustrations, Vernon Brejcha will do whatever is necessary to continue to work with glass.

Stripped to the waist, sweat trickling down his brow into his beard, he pulls glass from a kiln and shapes it by blowing into and turning the pipe onto which it is attached. In the short time he has before the glass cools, he makes a series of quick, almost imperceptible decisions to determine the outcome of the piece. While most of what he does is intuitional, a part remains analytical. As in painting, it is a process of guiding things in the act of happening, rather than following a set of foregone conclusions. On the day that I watch, he creates a piece like an elongated teardrop. It is lean and supple and looks like a caress feels. For a newborn piece of art, it is amazingly sophisticated and finished looking.

Doing what Brejcha does is not an ordinary thing even for the boldly experimental artist. It is tense business. Hot, hard work, where success and failure are separated by a very thin line. No second chances. If it doesn't work, or if you break it, start over. The piece I watched him make has flowing horizontal

bands that suggest a rolling prairie. It is a theme he has worked with over the years. In glass, it seems to undulate, to move and to express a vibrant life of its own.

Brejcha has a deep understanding of the high plains country of Western Kansas. He was born there on a farm near Holyrood, some 70 miles down the highway from Hays where he attended college and graduate school. When he enrolled there, it was the farthest he had ever been from home. "Drawing is very honestly the very first thing I can remember doing," he says. "It's all I remember." He drew in Big Chief tablets using crayons and pencils long before he went to school. His inspiration was the comic strips and he went through one of the big red and black tablets almost every day.

Sometime during his freshman year in college, he walked into a studio classroom and discovered oil paintings on canvas. It was his first encounter with a concept of art larger than the comics. The course of his life was set. There were friends and family back home who were worried about his decision to become an art teacher.

He saw his first glass art in a national ceramic, weaving and craft show in Wichita. He went back every Sunday until the show closed. Soon after, he resigned his teaching job and began a long, lonely journey into the emerging new art form.

Today he presides over one of the only university glass art programs in the area. He is a dedicated and highly skilled teacher. There is sound recognition from his peers and requests for exhibition pieces and lectures. He hopes that by now all those left behind in Holyrood know that everything has worked out for him and that all is well.

Blood and Dust, Hanging Dipper Series, 1984. Blown glass, 25″x 6″ x 5½″

"Drawing is very honestly the very first thing I can remember doing."

JANE L. EBY I met Jane Eby in a combination art gallery and frame shop in an old warehouse which has been given enough new layers of cement to hide its true origin. The handsome interior is gray, beige and white, a typical scene for places that display and sell art.

Jane was waiting for me and we went into a small gallery furnished as a conference room. It was our first meeting and I sat across the table, marveling at the combination of long, slender hands, luminous skin and serenely patrician face that looked like a Vermeer painting of a woman at a window, awash in golden light. Right away, I mentally put Jane in a wildly different environment: the marvelous clutter of the beautiful old home/studio that she shares with her husband, Randy Kust. Although I had not actually seen her in the house when I visited Randy, I had no trouble at all doing it. It was a perfectly harmonious fit. The old house with its gingerbread exterior and a young woman who could have wafted gently from the pages of a Jane Austen novel.

The walls of the conference room in which we sat were hung with large monoprints, a series from her exhibition in the gallery. She works here, she tells me, doing all kinds of things, from sales to administrative work to helping plan exhibitions. Although her voice is soft and low, its clear, even quality allows me to hear without straining. She has a studio at home and another over a combination pool hall, tavern and domino parlor on the west side of town. In her manner there is a sort of tough passivity, an unwillingness to let popularly-held misconceptions about art and artists slip by uncontested.

The idea of artists as simple-minded, fame-seeking romantics is absurd to her. The artist's struggle, as she sees it, is to find the best opportunity to think and to work with the least number of distractions.

She is wary of what the art capitals offer the working artist. Even though the art buyers, the art press and the art galleries are there, she knows that artists living in New York must spend enormous amounts of time and energy attending to things that do not directly contribute to the real progress and development of their work. For this time in her life, she is content to be in Wichita.

There is a directness, a kind of fresh new vitality that seems to generate extra light and to pump extra energy into the work. Monoprints are, by their nature, spontaneous and unlabored, but these reflect more than just the characteristics of the medium. She has elevated ordinary beach scene prints to important art by the bold, innovative use of color and a remarkable ability to suspend action in time and space. She also has the poetic sensitivity to use her craftsmanship in ways that do not call undue attention to technique. The innocence of the moment is made real and kept intact before there is cause for admiration, or analysis, of anything else.

Intellectually, at least, Jane perceives a need for themes in her work. Male dominance is one of these. It is a subject, she thinks, that can be easily observed on almost any public beach. In one of her monoprints, for example, a heavy-thighed male occupies the spatial plane closest to the viewer, blocking out a large portion of the background and clearly commanding the group of children working on a sand castle.

Jane Eby is a patient person. She seems willing to push ahead without demanding too much too soon. She is a leader and an active advocate for other artists. She writes, speaks and organizes on their behalf with quiet determination. I was struck with her apparent invulnerability to the small, petty matters of pride and protocol.

Outside the door, people were moving about, customers and employees. On the street, cars collected at the signal light, the drivers raced their engines and tapped their horns, impatient to move on to the next light and then on to the next one after that. The jangling, jarring, pushing, screeching, roaring sounds of a world in a hurry had no influence on Jane and our conversation. She moved on with dignity, speaking low, speaking evenly, a placid force for calmness and civility and consideration for all.

Beau Forte, 1986. Monoprint, 22" x 30"

Ronald W. Christ It was the last of November and from the windows of the art center I could see the cold, still day retreating into twilight, leaving behind the silhouette of black, bare-limbed elms and the frozen silence of the deserted Wichita State campus. Before that day, Ron Christ and I had never met, but I had seen his paintings and had spent sufficient time studying and thinking about them to have more than a passing idea of what he was about.

It's easy to imagine Ron Christ as the smartest kid in class, the kid who always has his hand up first and gives the right answer the first time. Even now, as he presses on into his early middle years, he seems to have all the answers.

As we sit and talk, he fields each question smoothly and expertly, snapping into it like an all-star shortstop executing a routine double play. He delivers flawless explanations to complex questions without a bobble, stammer or stumble. His manner is professorially crisp, his speech precise and pointed. There is a cool aura about him, not unfriendly, certainly, but detached.

His paintings are hard-edged, horizontal interpretations of land and sky. They are big and expansive and empty. No people. No animals. No cars or trains or airplanes or houses or anything man-made or artificial. There is nothing in his paintings to suggest that there is or ever was anything except the foliage springing from the earth, the horizon and the sky above.

Ron Christ's paintings are about nature, but at the same moment not about nature. He does not attempt to copy nature, nor is he sentimental about it. Its chief value to him is to serve as a catalyst; a way to begin an exploration into the abstract world of pure light and color, texture and form, weight and balance.

In his work there is a hushed, motionless quality, a split-second of time suspended forever. The paintings exist in a kind of ominous slumber, ready to spring awake in a great crackling chain reaction of unleashed power and

energy. It's like the pause before the storm—the angry, electrified interlude before a thunder clap.

Christ works by storing thousands of impressions reaching all the way back to his boyhood on a Missouri farm, often making sketches and taking photographs. Through these, he begins to invent a new image of the land and the sky. When he is finished, it will all fit into a harmonious, deftly balanced landscape painting that recalls Grant Wood's meticulously trimmed hedges and sharply delineated trees.

There is a deliberate innocence to these cropped fields, bare hills and the tightly configured shapes of trees and clouds. To many, the invented image will look more real than the real thing. It will open them up to deeper thoughts and deeper feelings. Ron Christ wants that. His work, he thinks, is like that of a symphony conductor. He sorts through a multitude of options, selecting, discarding, changing, searching for the right combination, seeking rationality and poetry, bringing everything together.

Orderliness and clarity and symmetry are common denominators in his work and in his life. There is a fine balance in the way he mixes poetic instinct with the mathematical precision of pure design. Ron once studied to become an architect and he still finds himself organizing space, seeking order through design. He also ventures deeply into the art of pushing believability far beyond ordinary limits through the use of sharply honed creative intuition. He confesses that when he is involved in the last and most final stages of a painting, the very small, very careful adjustments and changes he makes are all intuitive.

When he came to Kansas, he saw the long green ridges of the rolling Flint Hills country as an ocean. "I had never seen anything like it other than the sea," he said. "I lost all sense of scale. The hills seemed lyrical and intimate, but I knew they were huge. It was a stunning experience." He recalls the great horizontal masses with a sort of a dome for a sky. "That is very real and that's what I'm after."

Oblique Fusion, 1984. Oil on linen, 36" x 46"

It's like the pause before the storm—the angry, electrified interlude before a thunder clap.

BARBARA FRETS Day after day Barbara Frets spends time alone, working on large paintings of people—lots of people. She drives daily into Kansas City, Missouri, from her home in Kansas, as faithfully as any among the long lines of commuters streaming across the river.

She climbs three flights of stairs to her studio and by eight o'clock she has commenced to paint. She works steadily throughout the day until four in the afternoon. Ordinarily, there are two major works in progress.

She works in oil, applying the paint in thin coats on large pieces of canvas laid flat on a table. She begins with turpentine washes of color, moving ahead layer upon layer, using a technique which requires very little drying time.

Much of her work involves crowds of people gathered at ocean beaches or wading and canoeing in down-state Missouri rivers. There can be a dozen or

more figures in her larger compositions and each figure is done with a clear understanding of the natural inclinations of the human body. They stand, sit, slump and walk with the easy grace of real people moving about in vast oceans of space. Not much detail is spent on the figures, nor is it necessary. The large gestural interpretations establish the basic truths of the figures and their environment and your imagination fills in the rest.

Barbara Frets is a keen observer, a people-watcher with the creative intellect and draftsmanship to chronicle what she sees on the surfaceand below it. Like a Pieter Bruegel, a Hogarth, a Daumier, she reaches out to the world and presents the ordinary events of her time with candor, accuracy and sensitivity. She does not consciously include specific social messages, either of protest or approval.

Her very private artistic impulses govern what she paints and how she paints it. A realist in the grand tradition, she mercilessly edits out anything that doesn't contribute and adroitly moves the remaining elements about until a cohesive and rational order is achieved.

She is a highly organized person with a strong control over the processes involved in her work and her life. Her studio reflects her determination to clear away any distractions, any impediments to her work. It is located on the top floor of an old warehouse building at the end of Wyandotte Street on the northern boundary of Kansas City, Missouri. The ceilings are high and clear steady light streams in through a bank of windows which look north to the river and the old airport.

The studio is sparsely furnished. A huge vertical steel beam and the exposed pipes overhead are painted battleship gray. The walls are white and the oiled wood floors are uncovered except for a patch of loose carpet under her painting table. The entire building is leased to tenants with some connection to the arts. There is a gallery and an experimental theater in the building but Barbara Frets rarely visits the gallery, or spends time with her neighbors in the building because her work demands all the time she has to give. She is represented in more than 35 public collections and has been honored with a large number of prestigious awards.

She lets her work take her where it will. The beach series came about from vacations in Florida; the river paintings from family holidays. On the day of my visit she has just finished the third or fourth canvas in a new series on the ocean surf. In the new paintings, there are no people. What she is exploring now is the great energy, weight and force of the sea as it strikes land and rolls over the beach. It works. There is a strangely correct luminosity in the way the sun shines through the water, a perfect truth in the erratic rhythms of froth and running currents. I can almost smell and taste the salty, sun-filled air and hear the redundant roar of the sea.

Suggestion is a powerful part of the reality Barbara Frets creates in her art. Her personality reflects the strict orderliness, the deft editorial skills of the minimalist. She is intolerant of clutter and confusion or distractions of any kind. Every minute counts and Saturday is the only day free for errands, laundry and interviews.

July Sunday. Oil on canvas, 42" x 62"

They stand, sit, slump and walk with the easy grace of real people moving about in vast oceans of space.

SPORT
SWIM WEAR-1/2 OFF-SUN STUFF

Dale Eldred I didn't mind waiting for Dale Eldred. I had a premonition that he might be late so I bought a Sunday newspaper to pass the time away in case he was. I found the meeting place, a storefront studio in a kind of rundown neighborhood in the general vicinity of the Kansas City Art Institute.

I parked on the sunny side of the street and began to explore my newspaper. It was mid-morning and there was a procession of people moving slowly past my car to the drugstore on the corner which was about to open. As soon as it did, the small crowd that had collected at the door went inside. They seemed to come right out again, most urgently fumbling into new packages of cigarettes. On the opposite corner, a very old lady in a wheelchair was swaddled in blankets and wore a fuzzy pink angora cap. A handsome male attendant handed her a long holder with an unlighted cigarette in it. The toothless old woman rolled the holder around in her mouth, sucking on it, not caring that no smoke was coming through.

Not long past the original meeting time, one of Eldred's associates showed up and let me in. The studio was equipped like a large drafting room and is only one of several locations where Dale Eldred and his associates work.

It takes room and energy and a special vision to do what he does and to bring it into a rational focus. He works with celestial mechanics, the movement of our own planet and its position in the solar system. He converts creative impulses into scientific inquiry and back again into artful expression.

Eldred is a world class sculptor who works outside the realm of those who make statues. He has a passionate devotion to the creation of art that reflects the potential of physical forces already in motion. He often designs and installs sculpture incorporating diffraction panels to catch the passing, changing light from the sun. In Minneapolis, for example, he created a diffraction wall more than 50 stories up on a business tower. On a sunny day, people on the street below can look up and see a wave length of light, a phenomenon of pure light, the essence of light, visible in its prismatic form up to 22 miles away. The turning of the earth and the resulting change in position relative to the sun is visibly recorded on the sculpture's surface as one color fades slowly into the background while the succeeding color in the spectrum, bursts forth in brilliant, dramatic force.

There's nothing random in what he does. His work is about time, the fourth dimension as we understand it. His work on the Minneapolis Institute of Art functions very precisely with the passage of light that crosses there exactly at 12 noon. A red fluorescent light-reactive material is installed on the north face of the building. Across from it are two banks of mirrors facing south, set at

There's nothing random in what he does. His work is about time, the fourth dimension as we understand it.

exactly the right declination of the sun. At 12 noon, the sun strikes the mirrors and the mirrors direct the light back to the fluorescent board. The light then tracks across the board for five minutes for all to see. Viewers are actually watching the rotation of the earth. It's a very ancient ritual, Eldred explains, one that goes back to the Mayans and to the Plains Indians.

Dale Eldred gives off signals of great psychic energy, great physical strength. In college he was a football player, a discus thrower and a ski jumper. He looks like a handsome Michaelangelo with a broken nose. He has a long, muscular torso and a low center of gravity. His father and grandfather were shipbuilders and he looks like he could have been one too.

He speaks with absolute conviction and authority. His life is an odyssey among the giants of his time. He studied and shared ideas and concepts with Eero Saarinen, Minoru Yamasaki and Felix Candela. In his work and travels he has come to know virtually every leader in architectural design and thought. His cultural and artistic curiosity is unbounded by academic divisions. As a Guggenheim Fellow, he traveled the world unceasingly for two years, taking thousands of photographic slides, visually devouring everything at hand. He even sat in music composition courses taught by Aaron Copeland, and he has designed and produced the staging for three original ballet works.

He has gained virtually every recognition available in his field. He is scientist, artist, architect, poet and futurist. He is a Fellow at the Center for Advanced Visual Studies at M.I.T. and Chairman of the Sculpture Department of the Kansas City Art Institute. He is clearly an important voice, an important talent in shaping the way that we will perceive the world. And yet, here he sits on a mellow Sunday morning in an old storefront studio near 43rd and Oak, sharing ideas and experiences with a stranger. For all else Dale Eldred is, he is a wise teacher and a generous fellow voyager.

"I'm not interested in a sale," he says. "There's nothing in my work for anybody to buy. It's not available for purchase. Artists, composers, writers, deal in the most civilized act that one can make on the face of the earth—to give a gift to everybody. The most admirable point of view that I think you can bring to it is to go into your inner self. To realize, out of your vision. If you fail, fine. If you succeed, fine. But that's the real sense of it, of making art."

Kirkwood Hall Diffraction Floor, 1979. Diffraction grating and mirror plus sun, 80' long x 32' wide. Photography by Jay Maisel.

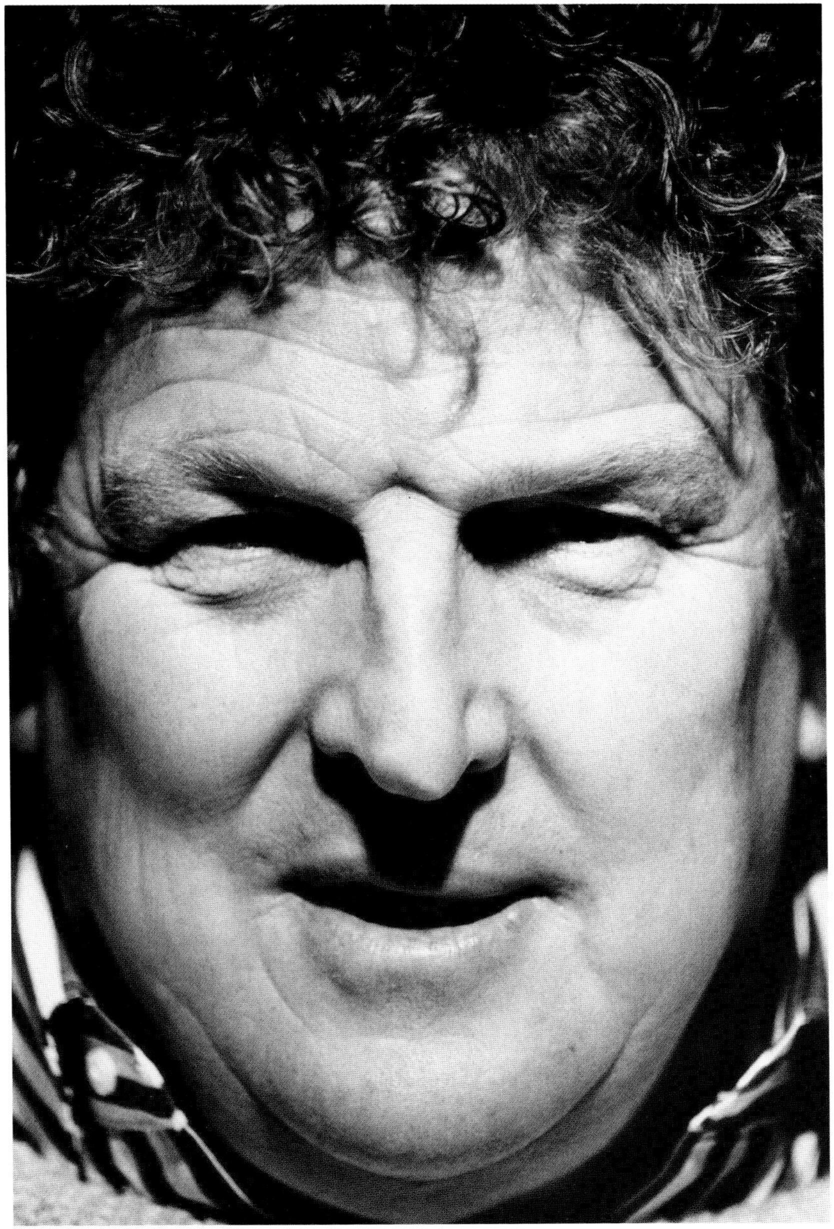

MARILYN GRISHAM The Grishams have a new house. It sits up high on a piece of the pasturelands that sweep down out of the Flint Hills, lapping at the edge of the city of El Dorado like ocean tides. The two-story Grisham house is nested in a cluster of single-storied homes.

It is winter and the marks of digging, raking, leveling and grading have been incised into the bare, frozen clay of the unsodded yard. The interior of the house seems to be one great continuing space, partially compartmented into individual definitions without actually interrupting the flow or the sense of unity.

There are lots of windows, lots of light, particularly on the lower level which features a two-story ceiling and space for those functions normally assigned to living room, dining room, kitchen and library. The bedrooms are on a mezzanine, the weaver's workshop on the basement level.

There are interesting and imaginative paintings and drawings from Africa and prints throughout the house. A very large brilliantly colored tapestry hangs like bunting from the mezzanine railing. Marilyn said that one of the most important house specifications was that there be room to display the textile from top to bottom.

Only a few pieces of Marilyn's work are included in the Grisham's art collection. Virtually all of her work is sold. In a great many cases, it is commissioned and the theme and size and much of its purpose is determined in advance. Marilyn is one of a new generation of fiber artists, successors to the artisans who made the tapestries that once adorned castles and churches. Today's fiber artists weave, but they are not weavers in the the ordinary sense of the word.

As a fiber artist, Marilyn pursues the aesthetics of her work in the same manner as a painter or printmaker. The creative considerations are the same. Fiber artists seek the sensitive inner core of an idea or image just like any artist. Unlike painting and other forms of graphic expression, however, fiber art does not lend itself to quick, spontaneous bursts of creative expression. When Marilyn works at one of her looms, she must set up certain things according to a plan. She can and does improvise, she says, but only after a pattern has been established. "The stuff has to stay together," she explains.

There is a strong air of practicality about her, a clear, even-handed ability to manage many details all at the same time. She talks easily about what she does as a craft. And says little about the drawings and studies she makes in preparation for her major work. She disclaims either the interest or the ability to be a painter but the skill and sensitivity shown in the small pastels demonstrate that she could be if she chose.

Fiber art becomes art through its creative content, she explains, but even so, fiber art can be both decorative and utilitarian. "If a work of fiber art becomes a garment, it's still art," she says.

Her studio workshop is alive with an incredible assortment of color and texture. Several shelves are crowded with spools of yarn in deliciously sophisticated colors. Raspberry and watermelon and cherry and grape and orange. And red, and corals and rusts and blacks and elegant pastel mauves and pinks, cool blues and grays. And there is unfinished work to see and piles of yarn and small sketches to show the origin of the ideas.

Her studio is as tidy as a weaver's workshop should be; but it suggests a feeling that something is simmering, that a sort of explosion of work is about to happen.

Many of the small, matted sketches are studies of the Flint Hills country. Translations of these make up a large part of her fiber art. It is not a confining subject. Her landscape themes range from highly imaginative abstractions to lyrical interpretations of sky forms. In *Wind Images*, she even manages to suggest extremely realistic landscapes from a layering of undulating land and sky shapes.

She is a remarkably energetic, forceful and productive artist with a keen and sensitive creative second sense. In college, she studied ceramics and almost accidently discovered weaving and fiber art. Now she is on the leading edge, exploring an ancient art form from a fresh perspective. Marilyn Grisham can't wait to get the looms moving in her new house.

The Rain Falls Mainly On The Planes, 1986. Woven tapestry with needle embroidery, 58"x 59"

Joan Foth Confidence clings to Joan Foth. Although she works in what is unarguably the most temperamental of media on an impossibly large scale, she gives off an aura of never having to sweat out the results. The drawing board on which mural size watercolors are affixed is so large and heavy that she must have the help of a system of counterweights to move it. In a medium which was for most of its history confined to a sheet of paper not more than three feet in its largest dimension, she now works from a roll of watercolor paper that allows end-to-end dimensions of ten feet, or even longer as she may decide.

There is virtually no hesitation in the way Foth talks, moves or interacts with people. She can extemporaneously express a difficult concept clearly and cogently without indecision or a need for repetition. When she is interrupted, she listens patiently until it is time to pick up on her last word. Then the two ends of her dialogue click smoothly together and the conversation flows on.

She seems to have mastered the art of the overview. Her artistic statements are tributes to the orderliness and rationality of nature. She paints in great sweeping panoramas, but the mystery she probes lies in the smaller subtleties of elusive rhythms running with the light across the rims and canyons of the western mountains.

Foth is also an accomplished draftsman and an intuitive designer. She works tirelessly to get the drawing for a painting just right and she may re-explore and redraw the surface as many as four or five times before the rhythm feels right. "When this begins to happen, when I know the design is going to work, then I can let go and be free," she says.

". . . in the Southwest," she writes in one of her papers, "the arid, cloud-refracted light changes so rapidly that a whole new set of forms may appear in

seconds. Colors change in minutes. When people ask me how long it takes to make a given painting, I can only say that it takes as long as it takes to distill so many choices into a coherent image. Sometimes it's a month, sometimes it's three years. So even though the forms are recognizable, the painting is put together as an abstraction. I think all paintings are abstract. Nature is never so obliging as to let you sit down and copy her."

Foth uses the traditional techniques of the watercolorist and makes the most of them. She first lays down transparent washes, carefully proceeding from the lightest to the darkest values. Nothing is covered up with opaque paint.

Foth's paintings sing out in the joyful language of mountains and deserts and incredible space. There is a tough, muscularity to the rolling, twisting forms and a quietness to the delicate clarity of the transparent skies.

She paints the Sangre de Cristos as Walt Whitman might have written about them. "Here, mountains are not only sacred," she comments, "but their chaotic, volcanic energy makes me feel as if I have dropped in just a few days after their creation."

Though her roots are in the east coast intellectual community, she perceives the world through a westerner's eyes. After many years in Kansas, she and her husband celebrated their twenty-fifth anniversary with a trip to New Mexico. It was then that she discovered a deep passion for the undulating forms and the rhythmic inner structure of the rocky spine that divides east from west.

In the years since, she has absorbed the look and feel and mystique of the empty lands of the Southwest. It is now her country and she understands it. She works and exhibits in Santa Fe with great success. Her children are grown and her husband is dead. She has the use of a studio in Chimayo, New Mexico, high in the blue-black shadows of the mountains.

Foth also works in her studio home in Topeka. Several times a year, she drives alone to Santa Fe, enjoying the solitude and the space and the peace. From the perspective of one of her own paintings, the car would be a tiny speck, pushing on to the south and west, moving towards the sun.

Mt. Taylor - Evening, 1986. Watercolor, 28" x 88"

"Here, mountains are not only sacred, but their chaotic, volcanic energy makes me feel as if I have dropped in just a few days after their creation."

Mt. Taylor – Evening

NORMAN GEE He no longer thinks in Chinese. Cantonese was the chosen language of Norman Gee in the household of his parents when he was growing up in the San Francisco Bay area. Now, after 20 years in a Kansas college town, he can understand most of the Cantonese he hears, but the old ability to speak, to see and to think in Chinese is gone.

Since his birth in Oakland in 1943, he has moved farther and farther from his ancestral heritage. His home in Lawrence is 1,500 miles from his boyhood home in California. And it is thousands more miles from the coast of China. It is as though he is living on an island on a great sea of grass. The barriers are formidable. The passage to the Pacific is blocked by high mountains and hot deserts and the highways west are long and lonely.

When Gee first came to Kansas, there were only a few Asian students on campus and an even smaller number on the faculty. Norman relied on books, pictures and an occasional trip to the Pacific Coast or beyond to keep alive the images of temples and tapestries and costumes and the ornate pageantry of ancient celebrations that floated through his mind.

Somehow, the richly embroidered symbols and decorations, the supple lines and misty landscapes, the majestic look and feel of walled cities and grand palaces, and the mysterious ambiance of older, wiser civilizations seeped into his paintings. His work became a strange and arresting combination of ceremonial subjects caught and held in a soft surrealistic dream-cloud.

We are in his studio on campus, looking at his new works. It has been a year since we last met and I'm eager to hear of the six-month sabbatical, most particularly the part about his trip to China with his brother and his mother.

They embarked for Hong Kong, then on to Beijing. In August the capital city was hot and humid, very much like Lawrence in summer. "It even smelled the same," Gee said. From Beijing they made their way south by train, bound for the village of his mother's family. A half-century had passed since his mother had left the mainland of China. She departed as a young woman of 20 and was now returning at age 70 with some understandable apprehension. The village was small, almost hidden in groves of banana trees in a sub-tropical rural district. His mother was worried about their ability to adjust to the primitive conditions and had planned only a brief visit. But the village was beautiful and the family home was a sturdy, handsome brick dwelling. The people, some of whom were distant cousins, greeted them with warmth and affection.

For Gee, the experience was an immersion into a world he had always imagined but had never experienced. The sights and sounds and texture of life around him permeated his senses. He visited museums and temples and

marketplaces. He began to develop new and deeper feelings for China.

A month later, Norman was back in the Bay area sorting out his experiences in a rented painting studio. During his stay there, he visited his father in a nursing home and made contact with one of his first art teachers, now retired. It was another homecoming, a re-entry into a familiar culture. And the new paintings began to evolve.

They seem to have moved to a more intense, more emotional level. There is a mystical quality about them akin to meditation. Even though the subject material is not new to him, there is a strange and unearthly quietness in the mood of the paintings of the post-China visit. If you look long enough, there are distant sounds of ancient Chinese musical instruments and the song of a nightingale may drift from a willow tree.

As we sit and visit, I notice again the quiet, graceful demeanor of Norman Gee. He is a product of cultures separated by thousands of miles and tens of thousands of years of history. From all of this has come a painter of rare poise and power, and someday he plans to go back and paint in his mother's village.

Maiden With Peach, 1988. Oil on canvas, 24" x 28"

It is as though he is living on an island on a great sea of grass. The barriers are formidable.

RICHARD GILLESPIE The memory is still clear to Richard Gillespie of the old man pushing his cane into the soft soil of the river bank; then he removed his hat and put the hat on the cane. Richard talked to the man until he was called home and when he came back an hour later, the old man was gone. The hat and cane were still standing there, a stark memorial to the lonely soul who had walked away from life into the dispassionate river.

Richard Gillespie was ten years old at the time. Death and drownings were no strangers to him. He lived between Third and Fourth Streets in Kansas City, the last stops to the bank of the great brown Missouri River that divides the city into two parts. He was often summoned to the banks of the river by the sirens of fire trucks as they roared off to discharge skiffs carrying men with grappling hooks. People often fell in or jumped in and the river closed over and moved inexorably on. Dark, brooding packing plants, places of death themselves, hovered over the river. The death themes which now rise to the surface in Gillespie's thoughts may well be in response to the sounds of sirens and the mournful landscapes of his youth.

There were also happy times during Gillespie's growing up. His mother was Croatian and his neighborhood was the celebrated Croat settlement known as Strawberry Hill. And even though his world was dominated by river barges and glimmering, criss-crossed strips of railroad tracks and large, windowless industrial buildings, he also remembers the color and pageantry of the Croatian culture. Back then, it seemed commonplace.

Gillespie delights in the recollection of the rugs that his mother made with the help of an aunt who brought home bright remnants of cloth from her job in the garment district. He recalls, too, that drawing seemed to be second nature for him. Eventually, he felt that it was also his life and he went across the river to attend the Kansas City Art Institute.

After graduate school at Stanford, Gillespie came back to Kansas City to begin life as an artist. In all the time since, he has never faltered in his conviction that making art for the sake of making art is the most important contribution he can make with his life.

Gillespie's work is highly disciplined, painstakingly difficult to execute and avant garde. He works with sheet steel guided by meticulously detailed drawings. The place where he works is clean and orderly with tools in place and equipment ready for service. It smells of cutting oil. Except for a large metal sculpture in progress of a reclining figure that looks something like the Tin Man in *The Wizard of Oz,* the place has more of the ambiance of a machine shop than an art studio. But it does match the sort of person Richard Gillespie appears to

be: strong, determined and skillful, both an accomplished artisan and an inner-driven artist. He has always been around machine shops and foundries, he says, and has long admired people who work with tools and machines.

Gillespie is a practical, realistic man and a working pragmatist. The work he does may be admired as much for its workmanship as for its poetic content. Upon close observation, it tends to produce a sense of something going on beyond the horizon and beneath the surface. It suggests that much of what Gillespie saw and felt as a child influenced the feelings now being released through his work.

There are people who are enthusiastic about the art he makes, he says, but they must be aggressive about seeing his work and purchasing it. To Richard Gillespie, a draftsman and sculptor of unique scope and perception, there is more to art than money or fame. That turn of mind is fortunate for him because during the more than ten years of service on the art faculty at the University of Kansas, he estimates that he has sold only four drawings and not one piece of sculpture. He believes this fact speaks more of his lack of aggression in seeking markets and patrons for his work than it does for the inability of his art to attract favorable attention.

He says he is not hostile towards conventional success nor is he angry with the operators of commercial art galleries, museum directors, or others who promote the popularity and sale of art work. For him, he says, the best approach to exhibiting is to do so cautiously and selectively. "We all need some strokes," he says, "and some acceptance of ourselves and our work. But I find it necessary to be very specific and particular about how I present what I do. Since I don't make my living making art, I can afford to be as careful as I am," he says.

"I really don't know about it," he told friends when asked about a review of one of his rare gallery showings in the influential *Art News* magazine. "Well, what happened?" they asked. "Nothing," he replied. "My life continues."

U.S.S. Coal Bucket, 1983. Sculpture, welded steel, 96" x 72" x 24"

Thomas Patrick Gormally On the day that I meet him, Tom Gormally is at a crossroads in his work and he is nervous about it. Unlike artists who travel down familiar roads, he is stepping into a dark landscape of shadowy bumps and mysterious shapes and half-lit dreams. This is the way it must be for Tom Gormally. The path he has chosen to take has little or nothing to do with making images that amuse or pacify or decorate. He makes only serious art intended to illumine the darker places in human nature.

His work is still in transition, he tells me, as he gestures toward a painting of a head of a black man and a fluted Grecian column. He is hopeful that the direction is right, but it is too early to be absolutely certain of it. The painting is not sophisticated, but the power is there to overcome the awkwardness.

He shares his studio with three other artists on the second floor of an old red brick building near the downtown section of Wichita. The studio is about 40 feet wide and runs about 80 feet to the alley where it opens up to a view of the city's baseball stadium and municipal parking lot. The front of the building is all windows and faces one of the city's main streets. Downstairs there is a tavern which is frequented by old men from the neighborhood who meet here to play dominoes but occasionally move stiffly through a game of pool or snooker. The bartender serves beer and cooks small greasy hamburgers smothered in aromatic fried onions. For many years, the tavern was advertised as a shortcut to the ballpark.

The light from the north windows is abundant and of excellent quality. There are buckets and tables and raw materials of various kinds scattered around our chairs. Several of Gormally's constructions can be seen in the background. Some are made of wooden laths and twigs. Some use large stones. Others incorporate paintings. A stick figure astride an animal stick figure has a peculiarly lifelike quality. The thin, muscular tension creates an immortal moment, split away and immune from the ordinary passage of time. The shapes and spaces in the constructions represent ancient symbols, religious architecture, metaphysical references, life.

Most of Tom Gormally's growing up was done in Minneapolis. He remembers being the only kid in the neighborhood who could draw. In high school, teachers praised his drawing skills. But that's as far as it went. He joined the Navy and after a few years he received a medical discharge.

Then he drifted. In New Mexico he had a near-fatal automobile accident. He remembers waking up to the realization that it could have all ended right then and there. Thoughts of his own mortality caused him to begin to do something purposeful with his life.

He finished graduate school in Wichita in the dead of winter. At about the same time, the graduate students' studios were burglarized and all of his tools were stolen. With no tools and no place to work and no job, Thomas Gormally was out in the cold.

He took a job in the woodworking shop of a manufacturer of photographic sinks. The work was repetitive and unchallenging and as winter wore on, he became more and more depressed, more withdrawn. "I wasn't fit to live with," he said, "but in the spring my wife bought a set of chisels and other tools for stone carving for me and the sun came out. I went to work and I've never stopped. The images I make," he said, "aren't supposed to be beautiful. What they're made for is to dig up the things we're doing to ourselves and give us a chance to turn ourselves around before it's too late."

Two Roads Diverged, 1983. Acrylic on wood, 66" x 60" x 106"

He remembers waking up to the realization that it could have all ended right then and there.

LYNN HAVEL He looks like he was designed to run with the wind across an endless track of prairie grass. At age 40, Lynn Havel has a lean, steel spring for a body, a small head and gentle brown eyes. The animal he most resembles is a whippet. When he rose to serve coffee, he moved so quietly and gracefully that he was back with steaming cups in hand almost before there was time to register his brief absence.

Havel's studio is hidden away deep in a Flint Hills pasture near El Dorado. A guide is needed to even find the entrance. From there, the passage is through a cattle guard over winding car tracks pressed into the grass and onto the edge of a stone quarry filled with rainwater collected from prairie runoff. This pond, with respectable dimensions of about an acre or so, is contained by quarry walls which rise a few feet above the surface of the water. A shallow sheet of runoff water rolls over the quarry wall to the east, creating a pleasant little waterfall.

Half of Havel's studio is on land; the other half is supported by stilts over the water. The entrance is reached by walking through a patio area. Windows and a narrow deck wrap around the one-room building.

The interior is sparsely furnished but comfortable, clean and functional. A tape is playing Mozart. Pale amber daylight tints the air. When the sliding glass door is opened, it is so quiet outside that a single bird call hangs high over the serene greenish-brown water of autumn.

It is easy to understand how Lynn Havel can lose all account of time when he is in this place. "I come in early," he said, "and I sit on the deck, listen to the animals, think about things, and then I go to work. Sometimes I lose myself so completely that I go past the time when I'm expected home. And even then, the whole day seems to have disappeared in a flash."

The work that Havel is doing centers on the creation of abstract images which float on the surface of great, outsized sheets of paper. Beneath, there are layers upon layers of other images. All are sharp, jagged, attention-claiming shapes, juxtaposed inside diagonal structures. The images are constructed of pieces and parts of memory, of environmental suggestions, and from an alphabet of made-up abstract language.

The paintings are multimedia creations in which paint, ink, crayon and graphite are put down, covered over, built up and scraped down. The result is a surface which changes as the echo images below rise and infiltrate to the top.

This moving about between the surface and subsurfaces creates an overall elusiveness. From moment to moment, the image is never quite the same.

The paintings are more interesting, more challenging, more diverse than they are pleasant. There is a restless, nervous quality to them, a reflection of Havel's highly energized personality and the only way he has ever found to express it. Even as a small child, he recalls that he was instinctively persuaded to share ideas by drawing pictures with pencil and crayons. "I stayed in from recess to draw," he said. "And even though I never had an art lesson until college, I can't remember when I wasn't drawing."

Although Havel doesn't consider himself a disciple, he is committed to the broad freedom to explore which is provided within the tenets of Abstract Expressionism. He has made an intensive study of Kandinsky and other Russian constructivists of the early 1900s and he has other heroes such as Motherwell, Rauschenberg, Pollock and Kline. He does not, however, go to these sources for ideas. He believes it is enough to use outside experiences to more fully understand what is inside the artist.

"The environment where I work is clean and wholesome," he said. "It gives me what I need to seek and find purity in the way I express life."

Wind Echoes, 1986. Mixed medium, 29" x 23"

A tape is playing Mozart. Pale amber daylight tints the air. A single bird call hangs high over the serene greenish-brown water of autumn.

JON HAVENER There is real energy coursing through the muscular metal forms of Jon Havener's work. You can see it move from one supple form into the next, running straight, then twisting, then leaping across a space, then turning in a slow, sensuous dance. The energy stays in the piece, flowing out, ebbing back, constant as the ocean tides. Perhaps the energy comes from what Jon Havener has forced into the metal. But this doesn't explain the ultimate sophistication in what he does.

There is a timeless, classical quality to the great soaring movements in his work and an understated elegance in the smaller passages. What is true is that his work is highly physical. It comes to be through fire and forge, hammer and strength.

Havener is built right for the job. He is big and blonde and he looks strong—a model of what a football tackle should look like. He was an athlete in high school until an injury stopped all of that. Havener is likeable and articulate, although he says he needs reasons to avoid spending all his time at home and in his workshop. "I could be a hermit," he says, "except for the teaching I do." His home is comfortable and appealing—a sunny pleasant house on a quiet street. His wife, a one-time classmate, is also a practicing artist. They have a baby son and a large, friendly dog.

There is no outward indication that Jon is a complicated man, and yet there are things in his work that say he must be. On the day of my visit, he had three major projects underway and an uncounted number of smaller pieces in progress. He must have several things started to keep the body of his work moving forward, for while he is doing one thing, it will very often suggest something for another.

There seems to be a connection through all that he does. He feeds on materials and ideas and takes advantage of what happens. Although he accepts kinship with those who construct things from found objects, the essential difference is that he makes the objects that he uses in his own constructions.

His execution of even the most complex subjects is flawless, a tribute to his highly professional training. He treats metal as if it were clay, ignoring its rigidity and insisting that it perform the same subtle transitions in shape and form without compromise. He has worked with it long enough to select a shape and see in it the endless variations there and when something he is doing stops working, he walks away, confident that its stored energy will keep it alive until he is ready to take it to the next level.

Havener has traveled widely, visiting the sites of ancient civilizations, collecting clues and scraps of ideas. His work demonstrates a deeply poetic,

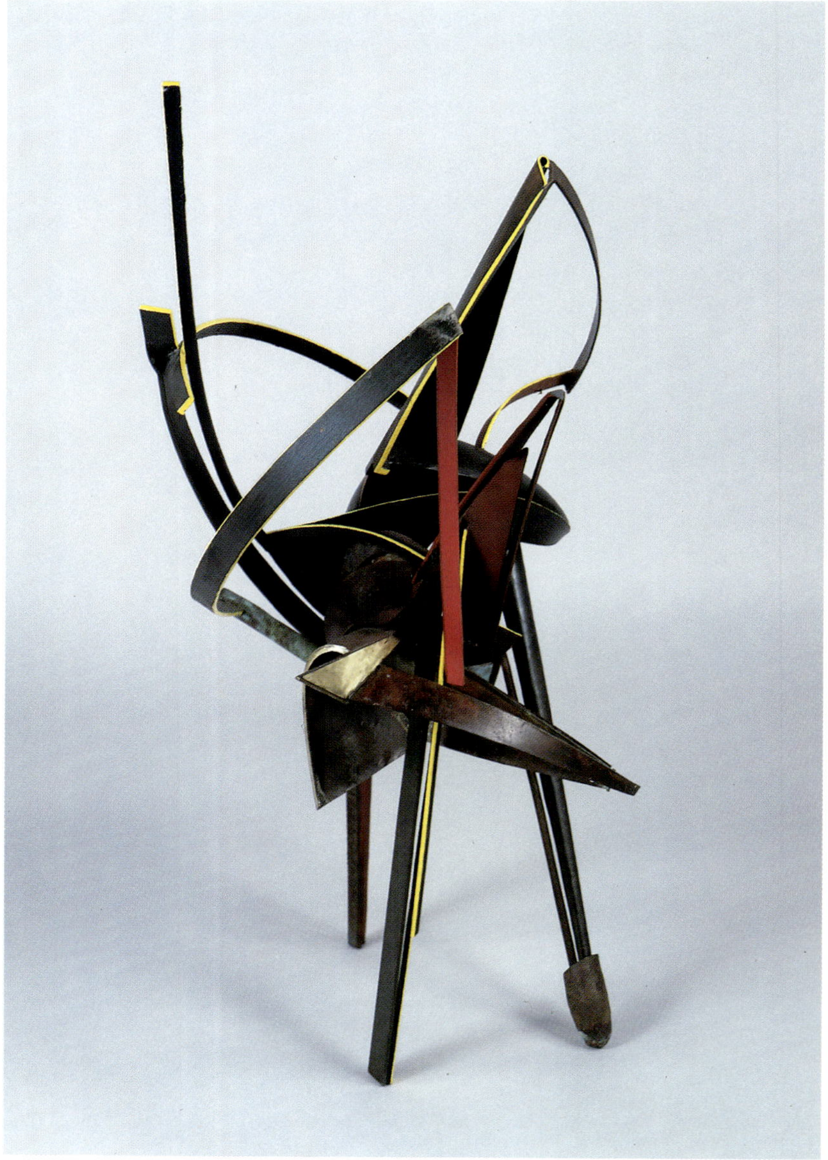

romantic nature and while it is ornamental, it is also filled with a kind of shadowy mystery, a sense of more to see and feel than what immediately meets the eye.

If you look at his work long enough and hard enough, you'll begin to think that you recognize some of the pieces of the puzzle. But the images are elusive. They dart around like minnows in a bucket. After a while, however, you begin to feel comfortable with the thought of taking a very special excursion into a very private place. It's the trip that counts. The objects remain enigmatic. What they are and what they mean remains wrapped in layers of thought and feeling. It's for you to decide.

In the studio/workshop back of his house, he has everything he needs to cut, fit, shape and form brass, copper, steel, nickel or even gold and silver. He can weld or solder or rivet; he can grind and polish and set stones. He moves confidently around his tools, equipment and materials. Once, he said, he built a 12-foot long fountain-pool here and he has produced a large number of other unique objects, ranging from small pieces to a six-foot steel, brass and copper fantasy called *Crusade*.

To me, Havener's work is actually best described as jewelry. That's where he started and even though his major work can be measured in feet rather than inches, it still pays homage to its origin in silversmithing and jewelry making. Ask him about it and he'll tell you that his concept of jewelry has always been the manipulation of forms and materials on a small scale. Now, he is simply thinking bigger and working larger.

Electric Cadet. Steel, copper and brass, 43" x 28" x 19"

He treats metal as if it were clay, ignoring its rigidity and insisting that it perform the same subtle transitions in shape and form without compromise.

Nicholas Hill I understood the pleasure in his voice when Nicholas Hill told me about his new freestanding studio on three wooded acres in the Catskills. A long time ago I took a bus from midtown Manhattan to upstate New York. It was during the last days of an Indian summer and as we rolled through the Mohawk Valley, perfect pictures clicked on and off the window by my seat like photographic transparencies projected on a screen. I remember it all.

Nor have I forgotten the magic moments on the huge lawn surrounding the inn at Cooperstown where I lounged and watched the slow, downward drift of leaves, each requiring an eternity of waiting in the cool sunshine. There is a quiet, patient, gentle quality to upstate New York—a timelessness, a sense of history.

Nicholas Hill came to New York after eight years in Kansas, the longest single period of time he has ever spent in any one place during his adult life. Things have changed for him. The landscape outside his window is about as different from Kansas as anything can be. And he no longer dresses to go to a college studio classroom to teach. Now he has embarked on a career as a full-time painter.

He starts working at six each morning, and works steadily until eleven, a schedule set by a careful determination of the time of his most productive biorhythms. Nicholas Hill is committed to a serious development of his artistic potential.

The environment around Plattsburg, New York, seems very hospitable to that cause. He has already found a place in the network of artists working in the area. Acceptance and friendship are very important to him. The friends he made in Kansas, in fact, are the things he treasures most about that part of his life. The years in Kansas provided a vital part of his passage into artistic maturity. He taught and painted, explored ideas and traveled. There were frequent trips to Santa Fe and to other parts of the Southwest. There were other more ambitious journeys to the South of France, to Florence and to the great museums of Europe.

All the while, Nicholas was taking in the raw stuff from which future thoughts, impressions and ideas would emerge. Bright, colorful, inventive images that tell of his admiration for Henri Matisse, and a kinship to American painters like Milton Avery and Arthur Dove. The medium-sized oils on paper and canvas gain their subject material from in and around Santa Fe, Taos and the Sangre de Christos. The paintings are playful, profound and poetic. They

seem to have the capacity to fill in the blank spaces that exist between looking and seeing.

There is a faint stiff-upper-lip attitude of a David Copperfield about Nicholas Hill; a certain good-mannered approach to life, an aura of honesty and hard work and pluck; a stout determination to succeed, no matter what the obstacles. There is, in fact, a British connection. His mother is from Plymouth, Devonshire, and there are other relatives in other places in the United Kingdom. Growing up, he spent long holidays abroad with his maternal kin. After college, he taught there.

Nicholas Hill is demonstratively honest in the gratitude he shows for the way things have gone for him in his career. There are no regrets, no serious disappointments, no apparent hidden doubts—only the urgency to move ahead with as little distraction and as few interruptions as he can manage. Today, he can feel all of this coming together. But there is still a long journey of discovery ahead for him. As the soft morning light breaks over the ridges of the hills, he is deep into his own visions of stored-up memories of Kansas. He is on his way. A path followed by painters everywhere.

Indian Queen of Portobello Road. Oil on paper, 25½" x 41½"

The paintings are playful, profound and poetic. They fill in the blank spaces that exist between looking and seeing.

James Holmes I have never forgotten the film, *Grapes of Wrath,* mostly because of the character of Tom Joad. The way Henry Fonda played him, he was strong and resolute and full of the quietness of a man who has learned to take what comes to him with patience and dignity. He wore the loose overalls, heavy shoes and coarse cap of an ordinary working man, but among his kind his voice was heard above all others. He epitomized the outsider; the one who wore no man's collar; the one we admired most, but understood least.

I think there's a lot of Tom Joad in James Holmes. Holmes speaks in a plain, matter-of-fact voice, while his eyes stick steadily on your face. He is strong and wiry, like one of Van Gogh's peasants. He dresses in tough, serviceable clothing and appears to be capable of lifting heavy loads and enduring long hours of hard labor. Holmes does, in fact, earn his living by working part-time as a carpenter. The rest of his hours are spent in the development of his career as a sculptor.

James Holmes does not operate inside any of the classic traditions of sculpture. He also avoids direct connections with contemporary trends in three-dimensional art. Even his own constructions fail to follow one another. What James Holmes does best is to avoid being ordinary.

His small home is filled with wonderfully strange art objects, some of which he has made, some found, some created by others. All demonstrate that life need not be commonplace. A pair of wing tip shoes, for example, are carved out of wood, covered with sheet lead, mounted on a shoe store display pedestal and given the title, *Lead Wings.* Another sculpture, *Rack Slouch, Bias,* is a toy house pushed into a parallelogram shape, apparently by the force of the wind.

There is a simple, direct honesty to the subjects and shapes and statements Holmes makes but they are not naive. There is an unsteady tilt to their meanings; a carefully calculated uneasiness in their balance. "I know what I'm doing," he says about his work, "and although there is a lot of whimsy and humor, there's more to it than just a one-liner or a sight gag."

James Holmes is indeed a clever craftsman with a deep intellectual and emotional grasp of what art can do. The lack of decoration and the spare manner in which he cuts, bends, carves and molds such materials as linoleum, wood, lead, paper and neon is almost minimalistic, but the end result provokes much more profound and complex responses. Holmes doesn't deny that he hopes for a more serious response to his work, but he also refuses to apologize for the humor which accompanies it. "Funny is better than sad," he says, "and anything is better than boring."

Although Holmes leads a simple life, he is not a simple man. He is, among a great many other things, a serious scholar of Kansas folk art. His woodworking skills have progressed from simple construction carpentry, on through a period when he set up and operated the common shop for the Kansas University School of Visual Arts, to his present occupation as an expert in the restoration of woodwork in old homes.

Today, after earning degrees from Kansas University and the Art School at the Chicago Art Institute, he is comfortable making art part of the time and working as a carpenter the rest. In school, his ideas of what he wanted to do in art never quite matched the direction the curriculum took and teaching never seemed to be the way he wanted to travel.

Like the indomitable Tom Joad, James Holmes knows the price of standing alone. He regularly commutes to Los Angeles to work on carpentry projects and enjoys a growing reputation for his skill as a restorer. "It ain't art," he observes laconically, "but it ain't bad."

Captain's Chair, 1981. Oak and steel, 26" x 50" x 18"

His eyes stick steadily on your face. He is strong and wiry, like one of Van Gogh's peasants.

MICHAEL FLORIAN JILG The tie he was wearing was one you would either love or hate. It was medium wide and covered by a splashed-on design in aqua and pink and Prussian blue. Although it appeared to be handpainted, it probably was a textile print. At any rate, it hung straight beneath Michael Jilg's chin, bobbing up and down as we visited like a floating exclamation mark. The name Jilg, he told me, is Czech and can be pronounced all in one syllable by changing the "J" to a "Y."

Michael Jilg first came to Fort Hays State University in Hays years before, a typical western Kansas boy with fast cars and beer drinking on his mind. Now, he is back again, a serious artist and teacher, preoccupied only with creative thoughts.

Jilg's studio is located over a beer tavern. At midmorning, the streets below are mournful and empty but the studio is alive with warmth and friendliness. Michael Jilg is clearly an open and trusting person and his amiability is contagious.

We plunge into conversation as spontaneously as two farm boys might leap into a swimming hole. I learn that at one time the studio was occupied by a physician, a bone doctor, who must not have cared that his patients had to hobble, crawl or be carried up the steep flight of stairs leading to his office. The imprints of partitions no longer in place and the different wall paint schemes left behind, present the studio as something you might see in an abstract stage design.

Work is in progress everywhere. Michael grins pridefully at the stack of drawings and matted prints and tiers of paintings hanging against the color-patched walls. It is the sort of sanctuary that artists crave: a cocoon of privacy, a quiet, obscure place filled with light, color and dreams.

The main studio flows into several smaller rooms which Michael uses for making frames, stretching canvas and storing paintings, equipment and supplies. This is a working place that bears layers of scars and stains to prove it.

Michael stands at a table piled high with drawings and prints, as eager to see them again himself as he is to show them to me. A series of etchings of Italian villages, streets and landscapes evokes a strange sense of familiarity, a distant echo from some forgotten experience. "People like them," he said, "but they don't represent the mainstream of my thinking or my art." He lifts the pieces away from the top of the stack in a careful, deliberate manner, like a man peeling an orange.

The impact of the large drawings he uncovers make them seem to leap from the paper. They are exquisitely developed ebony pencil delineations of figura-

tive subjects, mainly nude. Serpents, which sometimes appear in the heavy golden foliage, suggest an allegorical theme. The scale and the feeling of built-up layers of one drawing sequence over another is closely akin to the traditional oil painting and glazing process.

The draftsmanship used in the figures is impeccable and powerful. The textural detail is enormously imaginative and varied. "I earned a master's degree in nontraditional painting when abstract expressionism was virtually the only thing going on," Jilg said. "I became an expert in splattering, dripping, spraying and all the other methods for creating texture or pattern with paint without drawing."

Later, he said, he taught himself the more rigid disciplines of draftsmanship by filling large numbers of sketch books with drawings of landscapes, buildings and models. What he is doing today combines his virtuosity with pattern and texture and his mastery of figurative drawing.

Michael Jilg has boundless energy. The series of 20 ebony pencil drawings consumed an estimated 2,000 hours, a regular working year for a 40-hour per week employee with a two-week vacation. And that's just the starting point. There is also his full-time university teaching schedule, the every-summer research grant spent in Italy, the New York show he is preparing to ship, and the attention given to the dozens of acrylic-on-raw-linen paintings spread about the studio.

A cluster of small paintings, thinly painted on raw linen with their jewel-like images, glow in the shadows. A large painting full of bold, hard shapes sits finished on an easel. "I'm where I should be," he says. "I'm looking for something I've never seen so I can show it to others who haven't seen anything like it either. I'm a happy man. This is the life I choose."

Pruner, 1986. Graphite, 40" x 30"

"I'm looking for something I've never seen so I can show it to others who haven't seen anything like it either."

Cima Katz Even after 20 years, there are still things about Cima Katz that evoke memories of the counter-culture revolution in America. She has the self-assured poise of a generation that wore Indian headbands, sandals and mismatched clothing from surplus stores and made it an acceptable thing to do. She has the clearheaded sense of values that caused her generation to put materialism at the bottom of their list of priorities. And she still talks with the guarded quality of counter-culturists foresworn to trust no one over 30.

Today, Cima Katz shows no great interest in discussing the days when her generation took to the streets. She remembers that they were good times, especially for an artist working in an atmosphere that encouraged free expression and open thinking. But for Cima Katz, all that is over and done and unmourned. Even though she was a child of the sixties, her role in it was a passive one.

She has used the years since to study and to travel, and to develop a sharp and penetrating curiosity that has been with her as long as she can remember. The smallest fragment of bark or leaf or stem can grow into a very large composition of organic shapes swinging through graceful loops and arabesques, linked by mysterious fields of color and texture. It is always recognizable as something we know about but not something we can name, outright. It's all a part of her search for a new language; a way to express universal emotions and concepts and truths. She draws with paint and makes lithographs with great discipline, understanding—and highly practiced craftsmanship.

As a child in Westchester County, New York, she had the advantages of private art lessons, excellent high school art training and almost weekly excursions with her parents to art museums, galleries and concerts. After college and graduate school, she plunged straight into the process of being an artist. She traveled to Europe, to the United Kingdom, to Africa. She roamed across the United States, traveling light, seeing what there was to see; layering experiences, gathering herself up, creating an unconscious narrative and a personal, private alphabet—the essential tools of the artist.

As a wanderer, Katz is firmly rooted within herself. Once she moved into a cottage in Belgium which was filled with the personal effects of the last occupants. In a week's time, she says, she was as comfortable as if it had always been her home and her personal possessions. It is the same, she says, whether

she is in a house in Scotland, a hotel in Italy, or a cabin in Oregon. She is always at home with herself.

Cima Katz was 18 when she left her parents in New York. Today she appears as if she she could be a Midwestern farm woman. She is tall and strong-looking and handsome in a very honest, very natural way. She lives in a rural setting, not far from the university campus where she teaches lithography.

Her work and her life are richly varied and multi-faceted. She enjoys the society of her companions and music and conversation and conviviality. But there are times when she must be alone to read, to think and to peel back the layers of her subconscious in search of art.

There is a cool, formal elegance to her work. The drawing/paintings provide both a decorative feast and a serious minded emotional impact. The lithographs are cunning, clever and light-hearted. In both mediums, there is a depth of creative purpose that goes far beneath the surface.

Cima Katz is a rare combination of intuitive perception and graphic skills. She has mastered the ability to see beyond the obvious to the inner truth and to be able to put it down in a new and fresh language that anyone can understand. The trick, she says, is to think small.

I Can Get Off This River, Too, 1986. Mixed media, 37" x 37"

Dan Kirchhefer The headlights from my car are still cutting paths through the ground level darkness when the sun rolls over the horizon, spilling light, filling up the voids, etching shapes, fleshing out panoramic views of great oceans of grass.

The music on my tape roars into a huge, thundering crescendo, the empty sky is flash-flooded with fiery oranges and magentas and a long string of rose-colored cirrus streaks diagonally through the path of a jet's contrail. It's hard not to think of the third verse in the first chapter of the *Book of Genesis.* It's a spectacular curtain for a new day, sometime in March, somewhere east of Wichita.

I have promised Dan Kirchhefer that I will meet him in Emporia at 8 a.m. sharp and I make it with time to spare. Dan is packed and ready for a trip to see a Rodin show at the University of Nebraska. He looks like a young boy with a World Series ticket in his pocket, trying not to get too excited, trying to look cool. Not that going to cultural events is new to Dan Kirchhefer. Over the years, it has become a consistent part of his journey of discovery, his education, his coming of age as an artist.

The museum is a great teacher, Dan tells me, a way to sensitize your feelings; a method for elevating your understanding; a way to grow. He should know. He was born and reared on the vast prairies of Nebraska in the middle-sized town of Hastings. There were no art influences from his family's Mennonite background, no real art learning opportunities in the school system and no interest in art in his peer group. He was, in the matter of art, marooned on a tiny island of indifference.

His boyhood dreams of the future were vague and unfocused, except for the respect paid to his dead father's ambition to become a lawyer. His first few years in college were filled with listless attendance to a potpourri of liberal arts classes. He was generally uninspired until his first encounter with a college level art class. From that moment on, his commitment has been complete and irrevocable. The uncertainty of his career has been underscored by the twists and turns taken to get him where he is today.

Dan has earned degrees in Art Education, but now teaches studio arts. He is by nature an explorer; an adventurous traveler, a seeker of truth. He has a passionate interest in discoveries others have made; an intense desire to pay tribute to those who have left distinguishing marks in their progression through art history. He pays homage in very deliberate, very humble ways. In some cases, there will be an interpretation of an old print, such as *Death and the Miser* by Hieronymus Bosch, incorporated in his own work. In others, regard is shown

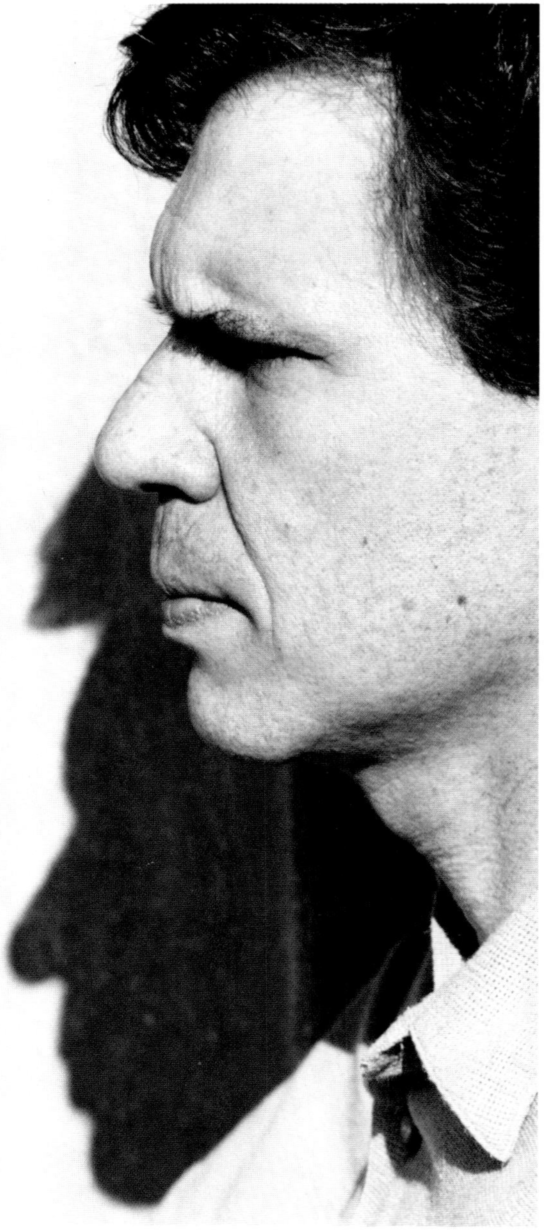

in the retelling of Biblical parables in very simple, but often enigmatic rebus symbols.

Dan is fascinated and inspired by how much Rembrandt got out of the Bible. He acknowledges that he thinks of himself as a moralist interested in gently revealing the foibles of everyday life. He considers the Biblical fall of Adam and Eve as the most human of all our experiences. Aside from the homage he pays to other sources, his prints have a pure and original credibility all their own. The strong, straight-forward etching technique reveals a sense of honesty; a candid, very intimate thought process.

The delicate spiderweb tracery of line punctuated by deep, velvet black interludes of tone and texture cast against large classical compositions make the 16" x 20" prints seem heroic in size and scale. It all seems to come from a special kind of austerity; a clean, laid-bare look that tells all in the most innocent of voices.

The work and the man are well matched. Kirchhefer is quietly unassuming about his art and its origins. He is only grateful that it is his lot in life to be an artist, to be a part of it all. "It's almost like a daily prayer," he said, with respect to Delacroix who said it first.

Pride of series *Seven Deadly Sins*. Etching, 5¾" x 7¼"

Silvia Kolyer The graduate exhibition of Silvia Kolyer was hung by others, mostly people from the MFA program for painters and printmakers at Wichita State University. When I visited the Clayton Staples Memorial Gallery at WSU, it was the final day of the exhibition and I was alone in the small, tastefully appointed gallery. The paintings were the kind of figurative works done in strong primary colors and values that have become the trademark of the German post-expressionists.

Characteristically, a single figure or two was included in an expansive field of color in each of the paintings. The figures were well-drawn poses, involving some degree of animation. There was a muscular quality, a feeling of live energy in each composition. There was more, of course, and I waited for it to come to me. As I circled the gallery, revisiting first one and then another painting in totally random order, I began to sense the same sad and lonely poignance that I feel when I hear the music in *Cabaret*. There is a bravura about them, long deep notes that hang on and on and on, reluctantly fading into memory.

I never met Silvia Kolyer. On the day we were supposed to be together, her husband called the art department and someone from there relayed the message to me that the appointment was cancelled because of a medical emergency. Silvia Kolyer had, in fact, been taken to the hospital suffering from a cerebral accident, a massive hemorrhage that struck her down without warning. The rest of her life was counted in days. What I know most about her was that she was loved deeply by large numbers of people.

When I met her husband on a bitter cold day almost a year after her death, he was still full of sorrow, still mourning in the way that people do when they keep asking "Why?" without hearing an answer. Paul Kolyer's voice was rough and scratchy and he looked to be on the verge of weeping.

Silvia was a native of Germany, he said, and a wonderful wife and mother. The survivors, he and a son and a daughter, had been proud of her talent and supportive of her career. Now that she is gone, all that Paul Kolyer seems to want to do is to keep her memory as alive as he can, for as long as he can. There is no animosity in his grief, only a heavy, unrelenting sadness. Even the speculation that the possible toxicity of solvents and thinners

used in her paintings may have contributed, or caused, her death is treated without rancor.

In talking with others who shared her experiences at the university, I find a touching tribute in the way that they seem to regard her as a fallen comrade. There is no sentimentality, only a sense of loss for the work that would not be finished, for the potential that would not be fulfilled.

As my meeting with Paul Kolyer ends, he hands me a single sheet of paper covered front and back with graceful handwriting. It is Silvia's statement for her graduate exhibition. In a way, it is her last testament to life and art.

Untitled, 1986. Oil on canvas, 30" x 24"

"I have always been fascinated by life's mystery and feel it's the element that adds spice to life."

I have always been fascinated by life's mystery and feel it's the element that adds spice to life. To me, art and image are synonymous, not in trickery but in making real what is unexplained.

The imagery in my work evolves from observation of my personal environment and investigates the mysterious nature and hidden meaning of the human mind.

My conscious concern is to orchestrate all pictorial details into a formal balance, preserving the physical and emotional overtones caused by the visual experience. In reducing and in simplifying the form, and in eliminating the nonessentials, I attempt to create an impression rather than true likeness and stage a mood that is worth questioning. The vitality and energy of the markmaking is an important vehicle by which my ideas and emotions are given visual form.

My working process is one of dialogue and discovery and a response to the sensual properties of the medium. It is in my struggle with the meaningless and in my intense effort to form a deeper meaning that my work becomes intellectually revealing, providing clarity and purpose to my inner self.

Silvia Kolyer

Margo Kren The large unframed acrylic on the wall of Margo Kren's living room is sensual and provocative. Ribbons of color swirl along a broad, circular path, twisting in and out of the black ground of the canvas. It's easy to read into what you see, the aura of a tropical night, pulsating music and exotic scents, but the painting began on an excursion into the Kansas rangelands. It is not a study of the jungle but of the elusive color and form of living prairie flowers.

For more than a year after observing the flowers, Kren filed their images away. Then, when she had thought about them long enough, it was simply a matter of synthesis—a quick, spontaneous outpouring of skill, knowledge and sensitivity. The finished work gives the appearance that it all went down with little apparent effort, without need to re-think, re-work or change anything. It hangs there, a handsome image, animated by an emotional intensity that must originate from several layers below the surface.

Without regard to any boundaries, Margo Kren works from one extreme to the other. She perceives no real conflict between abstract and representational painting and moves easily between the two camps. But her art is not always so easily expressed as the large acrylic seems to have been. Sometimes she must agonize and continue to work over and over a painting until it is right.

Kren does not completely trust her creative intuitions. She relies substantially on what she has studied, read and been taught. She pours enormous amounts of time and leadership into artists' organizations and is confident that the investment of her energy into networking with other artists benefits her own development. She is unceasing in her quest for artistic maturity. There is a bright, agile intelligence at work in her search. During conversation, she seems to be able to pick every idea out of the air, almost before it falls from the speaker's lips.

"I have always been an artist," she says. "From my earliest memories, my mother would take me to see anyone she knew who painted." Since her father was a Methodist minister, these were usually ladies from his congregation.

She traces the black in her paintings to the robes used in the church. She remembers, too, that the starkness and austerity of her father's church in Texas gave her an early craving for color and ornamentation. "I was drawn down the road to the little Mexican churches and their bloody little Jesuses with all the other statuary and bright color and the grave markers with the photographs on them."

In her visual vocabulary, black is female, mysterious and infinite, and she is comfortable and confident working with it. She has a passion for grand opera and can see an analogy between a blackened stage and the lights coming up and her own use of a black grounded canvas and the weaving of light and color through it.

Ordinary communication was often difficult for Kren. A reversal problem in her reading left her with a lingering mistrust of what she thinks she may have read. Her father and mother and sister and brother were not particularly verbal. Her art became a refuge; a way to express herself. Art also gave her the kind of status she needed to live up to her father's calling. From him, she seems to have acquired a sternly nonjudgmental outlook on life.

She refuses to state a preference of one kind of painting over another. "It depends on when you ask me. Everything does," she says. "Anyway, most often, questions of choice are unnecessary and inappropriate."

Kren is broadly tolerant of all kinds of creative expression. She is fiercely protective of her own right and ability to work freely in any medium and in any school of thought she adopts, without giving up one for another. "There's just a lot out there to explore," she says, "and that's what I do."

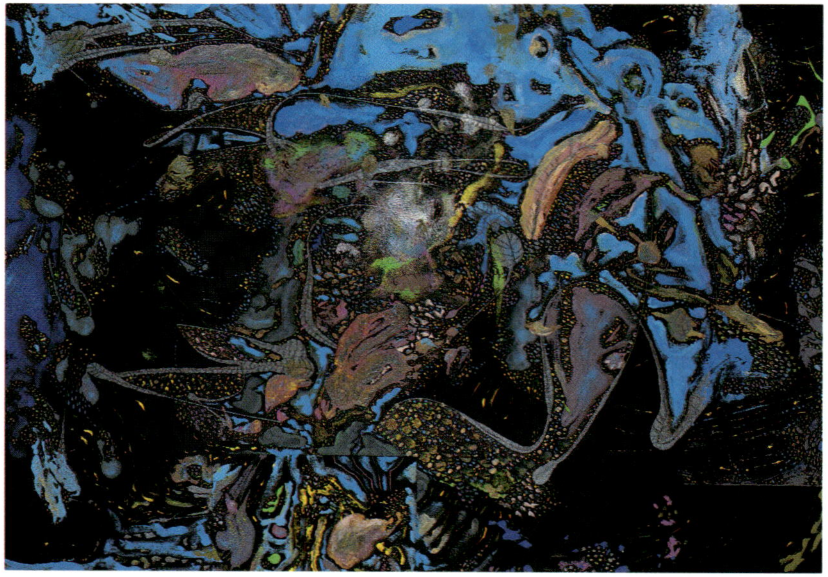

Race Between Two Appearances - Ragdale Series. Acrylic on black Arches paper 22" x 30"

KATHLEEN KUCHAR When she tells about growing up on the farm, Kathleen Kuchar's voice is lighty touched with nostalgia. She thinks about weeding and driving a tractor and feeding dairy cattle chosen for a 4-H livestock project. She sees herself working side by side with her brother and her father in the rustling, rolling fields of corn and soybeans that spread over northeast Nebraska like a green and brown and black quilt.

Kathleen Kuchar feels keenly the strength of the soil and the energy of the sun and the innocence of a life dedicated to planting and harvesting. She can close her eyes and see again her hometown of Meadow Grove with its familiar storefronts and people moving slowly and silently about like pale ghosts. She hangs on to the thoughts, the recollections and the feelings with quiet determination.

Since the death of her father, his collection of unusual neckties has become her own and she keeps it alive and growing with new acquisitions.The loneliness she felt when her father died has gone away. She is filled with the exciting possibilities of the ideas of making art that come without effort into her mind. They seem to flow in silently, gently, like silken seeds drifting on a prairie breeze. Now her life has taken deep root far south of where her brother still farms the family fields.

Kathleen Kuchar has become a painter, a printmaker, an abstract expressionist and an art professor. She works adventurously in any media that comes to hand or strikes her fancy. An experimentalist with boundless curiosity, she turns out collagraphs and color lithographs and glowing acrylic paintings. With a darkroom built into her home studio, she produces photographic art in startling varieties, including large Cibachrome prints and images created from manipulating Polaroid film emulsion. She uses her personal computer and a special software drawing program as a tool in her continuous search into new methods of image-making.

She lives alone except for Muffin, a 12-year old, almost blind poodle. Her cottage is neat and tidy and in good repair. She has added a studio to it and benches and tables and a fish pond for her backyard. There is an orderliness about her; a steady, balanced quality in her calm, measured manner of speech, a down-to-earth sense of reality that suggests that there might be more practicality than poetry in her basic nature. It was a thought that was reinforced when we talked about the work she was doing in color lithography; a medium that demands extreme patience and exacts a terrible toll for undue haste or for the most minute loss of concentration.

The idea of tightly registering several different lithographic impressions

representing a variety of colors on one piece of paper is a chilling thought to those who are only familiar with the relatively simple black and white process. But Kathleen Kuchar merely thinks of it as another kind of painting and follows the same basic technique. She layers one color over another, leaving bits and pieces of the preceding layer exposed. As the printing proceeds one layer over another, a fresh, spontaneous image emerges. In order for it to be successful, it must look easy and unforced.

In spite of what she might seem to be, Kathleen Kuchar is much more than an expert craftsman, a thoroughgoing graphics technician. She is a person given to spiritual thoughts, and visions come easily and naturally to her. She feels the emotional pull of color in a very keen, very sensitive way. In spite of her impressive reservoir of knowledge about technique, she is content to let her paintings and prints tell her what to do.

The result is not as abstract as it appears at first glance. She knows that there are biographical reasons for the shapes and forms and colors that make up the final image. However they may strike the viewer, the works of Kathleen Kuchar are very personal statements.

Debbie Aglow, 1984. Acrylic on paper, 23" x 18"

She is a person given to spiritual thoughts, and visions come easily and naturally to her.

MARGIE KUHN In autumn the older residential sections of Lawrence resemble a location in a college movie starring Peter Lawford. Leaves drop lazily onto still green lawns and a golden light washes over everything. There is a quiet, peaceful feeling that ascends high into the clear blue sky and covers the city like a cap. This was the nature of the day when I came calling on Margie Kuhn. She lives on one of those old streets where the houses are old and well built and used gently. It was the sort of house where the woodwork is covered with white enamel, the way it used to be before latex paint was invented.

The first thing that struck me was how small and young and completely feminine she looked. She reminded me of the girls in the forties and fifties with their shining clean hair and skin and their rolled up jeans and plaid shirts and other relentlessly wholesome qualities. She spoke in a soft, low, little girl's voice but there was clearly strength in it and a tough determination behind it.

We sat in a large living room with a fireplace and visited. There were some paintings on the wall, but otherwise it could have been a room in any one of the other houses up and down the block. She was, she told me, a member of an old Lawrence family. Her parents were both Kansas University graduates as is her brother. Her father is a physician, her mother an artist. Her college career was divided in two equal parts: one half studying biology; the other half in drawing and painting. As we talked, it became apparent that the names of Kansas artists, prominent in the past, that I dropped into the conversation had no meaning at all to her. But she paid ladylike attention, listening politely but without comment.

We visited the basement studio she shares with her husband, also an artist. There were finished paintings and others in process. Her husband's are all hard-edged, almost photo-realistic. Hers are geometric abstract compositions. The rough texture on the surface of the paintings is created by mixing sand into pigment and by building up impasto areas.

She is very self-assured in what she is doing. She already has spent several years doing representational images, mostly in watercolor, and she also has spent considerable time working commercially. She knows she can draw. And she knows she can manipulate paint mediums in the conventional, traditional way. The big, bold acrylic images don't require that she look at anything. She can now look inside her own imagination and draw from her own private musings. She is free to explore in a way that she had never done before. "People used to get so involved in who the person was, or what the objects were in my paintings that they missed whatever point I was trying to make."

She is so utterly confident of the direction that she has taken that she is working in wholesale lots. "I was trained to be a scientific illustrator," she said. "That's the reason for the biology." But when she learned that there never seemed to be an end to the amount of biology and other science courses she would need to succeed in that profession, she gave it up.

As I look at the luminous and very expressive rectangles and circles floating against the dark grounds of her canvases, I think of the potential that lies ahead for her. Her serious work is in the process of happening and I almost have to struggle to put down any resentment I might have for her youth, her energy, and the great amount of future still out there for her.

There is a certain feeling of inevitability in her attitude about the work she is doing. She seems to know that she is on the right track. It's like watching a gifted young performer in any field putting the finishing touches to skills and talent. Only time can tell.

Still Life, 1986. Acrylic on canvas, 20" x 24"

She spoke in a soft, low, little girl's voice but there was clearly strength in it and a tough determination behind it.

RANDALL JOSEPH KUST The simple house in Wichita is on an oversized lot, a part of which is converted to a vegetable garden. The large, bearded man at the door is Randy Kust. He smiles at me in the sort of abstract way that people do when they are looking at something that they alone can see. Randy Kust, I was to learn, does not have to seek inspiration. He is surrounded by it all the time. His pets, his plants, his dreams—all the stuff that his life is made from—are the sources for his work.

He gives me a tour. Drafting tables, printing equipment, files, framing and mat-cutting tools and stacks of paper, matboard and other supplies are strung out through the house. It is clear that the entire house is his studio. In fact, there appears to be very little separation between Randy Kust's life and his work. His state of mind and what he is doing at the moment are often catalysts for an idea for a print. And the print can then become a series.

As we talk, I get the feeling that he is speaking to me, thinking about something else and seeing beyond the room, all at the same time. He moves about, shifts his weight, jiggles his knees and occasionally taps the floor with his feet. I am seated on a high stool, looking around at Randy Kust's world.

The house is a charming clutter of old furniture, potted ferns and plants and partly finished restoration projects. It is warm and pleasant and friendly. Champagne colored light splashes in through tall, narrow windows and touches Randy Kust's face glowing with satisfaction. I imagine him working his way through his home, stopping here to do one thing, moving on to do another—every move choreographed into one grand performance.

We begin to look through a stack of prints. As we lift the individual sheets of paper, a fanciful community of odd creatures and strange symbols begins to emerge, page after page. There are sheep, cats, a solitary ram and fish. There are people and other things of indefinable origin. The settings in which they live are bizarre. They look like the characteristically empty moonscapes found in the vocabulary of surrealism. Many of them are starlit and the figures and other parts of the story float freely, independent of the laws of physics or of rationality. All of the sheep, for example, wear textile coverings over their own wool coats. A galaxy of little stars pokes holes in the black velvet universe in another. The effect is dizzying.

I think of Randy Kust's mind as a fantasy airfield from which squadrons of ideas, images and inventions take off and go whizzing into the air, taking the viewer along. Plainly, there are more things inside waiting to get out than he can deal with one at a time.

Randy Kust was born in 1948 in Green Bay, Wisconsin. He tells me his youth was mostly bright and sunny, broken only by intermittent dark clouds of anxiety. "I hated school," he says. "I was always afraid I wouldn't pass." The fact that he was the biggest kid in every class gave an extra sharp edge to his fear. There were no art classes in the parochial schools he attended. The only formal art experience in his classrooms came in the form of assignments to commemorate special days. "On Columbus Day," he recalls, "we would take our crayons and create our idea of the discovery of America.

Now, after years of studying and apprenticeships, he can do it all: drawing, designing, making the plates, printing, matting, framing, photographing the work, making shipping crates. He even makes some of the paper he prints. He also paints, sculpts and makes ceramics.

The art he makes is spectacularly confident. He quite literally does whatever he wants to do to achieve the effect he is after. He boldly mixes techniques from as many different printmaking processes as he chooses. And he gets away with it. He pushes reality to the outer limits without losing representational identity.

He tells me the story of one special print, a commemorative etching made to celebrate the life and passing of Monkee, the household cat. "After Monkee died," he says, "my wife, Jane, and I talked about what we thought had happened to him, where he was and all of that. So I made this print. There you can see old Monkee floating through the universe, reunited with all his other lives. This is my hand, and that is Jane's waving farewell as Monkee flies by over Kansas." The cat in the print has a maniacal grin. It seems very much alive. Monkee lives.

Home, Home on the Range, 1981. Intaglio color etching (four plates), 16" x 22"

ELIZABETH LAYTON Both hands fly around Elizabeth Layton's face like pretty white birds. They move in tempo with the conversation, punctuating and outlining ideas, tracing thoughts in the air.

"My family called me stubborn," she sighs. "I never seemed to be on the same track as other people." Before she turned to drawing in the seventies, she was a writer and a poet. Then she began to transmit the images that filled her mind and coursed down her arm and hand and through her pencil on to large sheets of newsprint. The lines seemed to fall magically into place, wiggling their way across the paper, leaving a trail of objects defined by their own special contours.

Her work demonstrates an uncanny perception for the selection and placement of precisely the right objects and there is a very sophisticated, very polished overtone to her drawings. Her work is far more intellectual and philosophical than decorative. She simply has a lot to say and an urgency to say it. The subject is always people. "I was hung up on women's issues for a long time," she says, "until I got it worked out."

Now Elizabeth is working out her feelings about hospitals and nursing homes and how it must be to grow old and helpless. Her sister was kept alive from July to October with no apparent purpose or hope and a 93-year old aunt suffers the indignities of life in a nursing home with no choice in the matter. "I'm doing a lot of thinking about old age and dying," she says, "and Glen doesn't like it." She turns to her husband and he gazes back at her. The gentle looks they exchange are filled with tenderness and admiration and respect. "Glen would rather go see a ballgame down at the high school." There is no criticism in her voice.

Elizabeth Layton has poured her own feelings into a series of six powerful commentaries which she has titled, *The Motherless Child.* She sits on the bed while we visit in her upstairs studio and she displays her drawings, one by one. The cast for each is a motherless old child and its attendant. Cables and tubes and plugs and restraints and other cold and impersonal things set the stage. The plot is simple: Unable to run away, the motherless old child struggles and strains and resists; knotted muscles twitch and twist and pull; eyes bulge and mouths contort—the last wild thrashing about of a human spirit refusing to surrender.

Outside, the sun comes from behind a cloud and light bursts into the room, creating a soft aura around Elizabeth. We move about the small room, looking at memorabilia pinned in overlapping layers to all four walls. There are snapshots and notes and clippings and drawings of valentines and rainbows. Downstairs, an even larger rainbow mobile turns slowly.

When we prepare to say goodbye, Elizabeth tells me that she is aware that her preoccupation with death and dying is an uncomfortable subject. "They are hard drawings," she admits, "but they are things that should be said. I'll get over it," she promises.

Remembering Names, 1987. Color pencils on paper, 30" x 22"

"I was hung up on women's issues for a long time until I got it worked out."

JUDY BURNS MCCREA When I was a boy, the neighborhood where Judy McCrea now lives was solidly middle class. It sat right on the fringe of a very wealthy area where many of the houses had pillars and gazebos and virtually all of them had live-in servants.

I can still hear the lazy clicking sound of hand mowers and the soft conversation of maids as they swept the porches and cleaned the windows and pulled fresh-smelling laundry from backyard lines. The whole world seemed like it could have been clipped out of the *Saturday Evening Post*: white houses shining out of deep lakes of blue-green shade; the bright clear uncomplicated days of innocence. That's all gone now. All that remains is a shamble of cruelly treated houses with peeling paint, swaybacked roofs, tattered trees and dusty gardens.

Judy's house is one of a few scattered restorations that holds on to any style and dignity. From the street you see a handsome and sturdy brick house with a small yard and clean swept walks. But it was a tired, termite-infested place when she bought it and, on her own, brought it back to life.

The house is important when you think about Judy. It is an object of her creative force; another thing that shares the focus of her skill and training and intuition. Painters like Judy taste the glories of creative discovery but they pay the price.

It's easy to see her as a power generator; a sort of cooker that constantly lets off creative steam while more is bubbling on the back burner. Her paintings hum with a sort of raw, lusty vigor and with enough strength and energy to overpower any sense of loss from understatement.

She paints in the attic, a magnificent studio full of interesting shapes and angles; slanting ceiling lines, shadowy corners, large open areas of hardwood floor, places to sit and look out the windows. There are benches, odd chairs and a sofa. Not a place to entertain in any formal sense, but a comfortable companionable place, exactly the right ambiance for working. Two large unfinished canvases, temporarily mounted on panels, glow with bold color and dance with large, figurative shapes. There is the beginning of life in both and a growing excitement is beginning to build.

Judy became a master of draftsmanship long ago. She draws with the power, precision and understanding of earlier schools of representational painting. There are things in her work that recall John Steuart Curry.

She has developed the skill, essential to all competent draftsmen, of suggesting muscle, tissue and bones beneath the surface of the drawing. A painting of a big white bull becomes an extension of the living, breathing animal. There is more to the image than a faithful copy. It is also a statement about weights, balances and harmony.

Judy uses classical draftsmanship as a point of departure from which to leap into certain elements of abstract expressionism. The combination allows her to explore multiple levels of thought, emotion and reality.

Today she paints, teaches, travels and thinks. Her determination to succeed, to move ahead, to make a mark is undiminished. By ordinary standards, she has successfully achieved the stature of professional painter and teacher. Her credentials are impressive; the list of accomplishments long and lengthening. But she is still pushing her goals upward.

Resurrection II, 1985. Oil on canvas, 44" x 48"

Nancy K. Means The country music that used to come wheezing out of the second floor dance hall on West Douglas in Wichita stopped years ago. And the shadow-figures of dancers clogging and jigging across the painted windows are gone, too. My friends and I used to sit on the curb and watch the silhouettes of dancers flitting from window to window like images on a row of television sets. Even as young as I was, I was sad to think that someday it would all vanish as if it never had been there in the first place.

I remembered all this when I drove down West Douglas Avenue looking for Nancy Means' studio. I found what I was looking for over a floor coverings store, not far from where I used to go to the movies, several blocks west of the dance hall. The stairs ended in a very large room, a kind of multi-purpose area that Nancy and the other artists in her group had planned to use for an art school. The school idea hadn't worked because there was no fire escape. Now that the whole area is included in a big development scheme, Nancy said, the landlord was not eager to renew their lease. "When the developers move in, the artists move out," she said.

The space allocated to Nancy is on the north side of the building and the large windows flood the room with good steady light. It's a neat and tidy place, but the gas heater has not been on long enough and it is cold. Nancy is small and thin, but her bright, sharp wit tells you to save your pity. She's tough, in the way that artists are called on to be.

Without experience or training, she won a job as a graphic artist with a large industrial firm on aptitude alone when she was 19. Years later, she studied painting at Wichita State University at both the undergraduate and graduate levels. Later, she wrote new chapters for the painter's guide to survival: She taught wherever she could—in special education, as a substitute instructor at the Wichita Art Museum, as a lecturer at the university, in private classes, and finally, as a commercial art instructor in a business college.

Nancy painted, exhibited, organized and worked at developing a market for her work. Now she lists page after page of competitive and invitational exhibitions, awards, commissions, private collections and positions in art organizations. This is her life now: painting and exhibiting and adding new entries to her long list of successes. The work reflects her deep and persistent interest in the holistic approach to life. She believes in the essential unity, the connectedness of everything in nature. Out of all this, she believes, comes a sort of cultural memory that allows things to pass through her own consciousness that she would not otherwise know about.

She gains a sort of omniscient point of view for her work by freely changing

from one eye level to another. She often moves up where she can look down like a camera on a high boom over a motion picture set. She adroitly captures the psychological essence of space, making you feel its presence, encouraging you to think about yourself as a part of it.

There is a mystical quality, a kind of cross between the somber, ghostly images of Albert Ryder and the laughing, wildly whimsical floating figures of Marc Chagall in Nancy's work. She crams light in and meticulously, cleverly employs tiny broken bits of calligraphy to break up the larger design spaces, small fragments of pure pastel that add life and energy to the surface.

Nancy consciously controls the emotional content of her work with strongly disciplined, highly developed design skills. She has a deep interest in what is potentially there, but is not there yet. She expects her mind to bring something special to every image, a passing thought, a piece of the collective consciousness. To that extent, Nancy Means lets her imagination run free.

Cosmic Coyotes in America, 1987. Oil pastel and acrylic on paper - Diptych, 38" x 100"

JIM MUNCE Here is a contented man. Jim Munce has no particular interest in the current events of the art world. Most of the artists with whom he is intrigued are dead. He likes the calm, even existence provided by his job as a university professor, and he has to go no further than his own thoughts to find subjects for his prints and drawings.

Munce finds even the quiet, ordinary, almost imperceptible rhythms of life about him as a source for his sense of well-being. His serenity is natural for the person who wants little more than he already has. The struggles of others to achieve power, prestige or possessions are irrelevant to him. He exists not to acquire but to think and to explore other dimensions of the human experience. He does so through his skill as a draftsman and as a printmaker.

Though not a religious person in the institutional sense, he is enthralled with the idea of God and with the Christian symbolism used to explain the concept. St. Francis of Assisi particularly fascinates him. "St. Francis is the least dogmatic," he explains, "and the most identifiable with the lives of ordinary people." St. Francis has been the subject of the largest body of Jim Munce's work for the last several years.

A large etching, *St. Francis confronting the Eucharist*, sits propped against the window in the small dining room. The setting is a made-up landscape that looks like something out of a medieval fairy tale done in rich blends of olives and greens. A pink moon hangs over the tableau, casting a hushed, dream-like quality over the cowled figures and the matrix of shapes and objects that surround them. It is a dramatic moment delivered straight from a profound response to a deep and moving experience with the subject material.

Jim Munce works that way. Even when he isn't concentrating on an idea for some specific image, his thoughts are idling, moving towards something, sometime. "One time," he recalls, "I sat on the front porch and looked at my wife's strawberry patch while I smoked a cigarette and sipped from a glass of wine. While I sat there, I imagined St. Francis urging the strawberries to grow larger and sweeter for the greater glory of God." Out of this came a series of prints of St. Francis preaching to the garden.

Munce draws with power and passion and precision. He works with confidence that comes from knowing he can do whatever he chooses. His drawing subjects often come from ancient statuary and architectural artifacts. Under his hand, they are filled with energy and life. In the early stages, his drawings are largely gestural—abstract marks indicating the direction and motion and placement of objects yet to be developed. "Drawings are done to see what they are going to look like," he explains. "Rigidly following a preconceived idea would be very dull and unrewarding."

Curiously, Jim Munce looks a great deal like the established imagery of ancient religious ascetics in general and St. Francis in particular. His deep set eyes, high cheekbones, classically sculptured chin and jaw and thin but sensitive mouth look like a meld of a thousand romantic versions of saints. Add to this his short, cropped hair with just a suggestion of a forelock which seemed to be the standard saintly haircut. If Munce is impressed with any identification with his subject material, he doesn't show it.

He straightforwardly explains that he came from an ordinary background in Sioux City, South Dakota. His father and brother still operate a moving and heavy hauling business there. There were no cultural pretensions. He simply grew up in a normal Midwest environment, finished high school and because there was no money for college, joined the Air Force. He became an artist because "I drew better than I did anything else."

Today, after almost 20 years of teaching, Jim Munce fills up his days with working and thinking and making prints and drawings. When he needs to refuel his imagination, he reads something from Kazantzakis or puts on *Mahler's Third.* His life is as complete as he expects it to be. "I have my work and my family and my thoughts," he says. "What else do I need?"

Resurrection, 1985. Pen drawing, 16" x 22"

John Newman I understand John Newman. He likes to draw. And so do I. When I was a boy I managed to draw with materials that were at hand, natural things that were a part of wherever I happened to be. Chalk rocks used for ballast in railroad beds were perfect for reverse line drawings on brick-red boxcars. Burnt ends of sticks worked well on the white painted cement walls of the huge pipe organ-configured grain storage bins. At least once, I used a granite chip to incise an image into a softer limestone boulder.

In more civilized circumstances, I found pens in post offices, pencils in church and crayons at school. Just about everywhere I dropped my hand, there was something available to slake my thirst to draw, to make my mark, to leave my spoor.

It appears that John Newman's passion for drawing is at least the equal of my own. He draws on a heroic scale. He does it in big, solid forms and in thin, energy-electric linework. He understands that there is something magic about drawing: One minute there's nothing there. Then there's something. A face, a figure, an object, an abstraction, a new image on the face of nature.

John Newman's work is dominated by an interest in creating an illusion of three-dimensional reality. There is a convincing sense of weight and volume and depth to his large figurative compositions; a transmitted belief that there is air and space in front of, to the sides of and behind the objects which we know to be flat and two-dimensional but choose to accept as the real things.

In order to do what he does with paint and charcoal and printing ink, he first had to acquire the ability to make the subtle shifts in line and tone, color and texture, that will easily and effortlessly cause a form to turn in space.

John Newman began to build those skills as long ago as he can remember. His first venture into art as a pre-school child was casting tiny clay animals from a set of plastic molds. He began drawing as soon as he could use a crayon or pencil. The urge to draw was as natural to him as breathing. It was always there, he says, a part of his curious nature.

When he started a drawing, questions about how to make it better automatically popped into his mind. And even though his mother was untrained in art, he asked for her help. Between the two of them, they would work out solutions

drawn from both logic and instinct and practical mindfulness. It was the way he learned to draw by matching up relationships. If it's too small, make it bigger; if it's out of place, change it; if there's more wrong with it than right with it, start over.

Without conscious determination, John began an empirical process of learning to draw, the traditional method followed by generations of the classical masters of draftsmanship.

Today he has combined countless thousands of trial and error lessons with the discipline of years of formal academic and studio training. He has reached the level where the line that flows from his hand seems almost to have a life of its own. His work has the sophisticated editing, the high energy tension, the practiced ease that can come only from a great reservoir of self-confidence. And from someone who has paid his dues.

Today, John lives in Ohio, teaching art in both the public schools and in a community college, sharing parenting and household responsibilities with his wife, a doctoral candidate in psychology. His home is in a quiet pastoral setting outside the college town of Yellow Springs. It abounds in hiking trails through woods and meadows. His studio is in a converted two-car garage. He misses Kansas where, he observes, "all you need to do to find a landscape is look out the window."

In the tradition of Daumier, Hogarth and Kollwitz, he finds inspiration in the world around him. A fleeting glimpse of a huddle of street people is noted quickly and spontaneously in his sketchbook. Later, he will use it to develop a concept for a major work, a painting which will require models with costumes and special lighting effects. The idea may come from life, but the creative strategy is his to control.

He has found ways to make statements involving tragic events in South Africa, black serial murders in Atlanta and the drowning of the Haitian boat people. He is deeply concerned and quietly determined to do what he can do with his art to address the problems of his time, but he remains more artist than social activist.

He finds a quiet contentment in the fact that the work he is doing as a teacher will imprint the future. He remembers all the help he received from wise and sensitive teachers—and is inspired to go the extra mile with his own students.

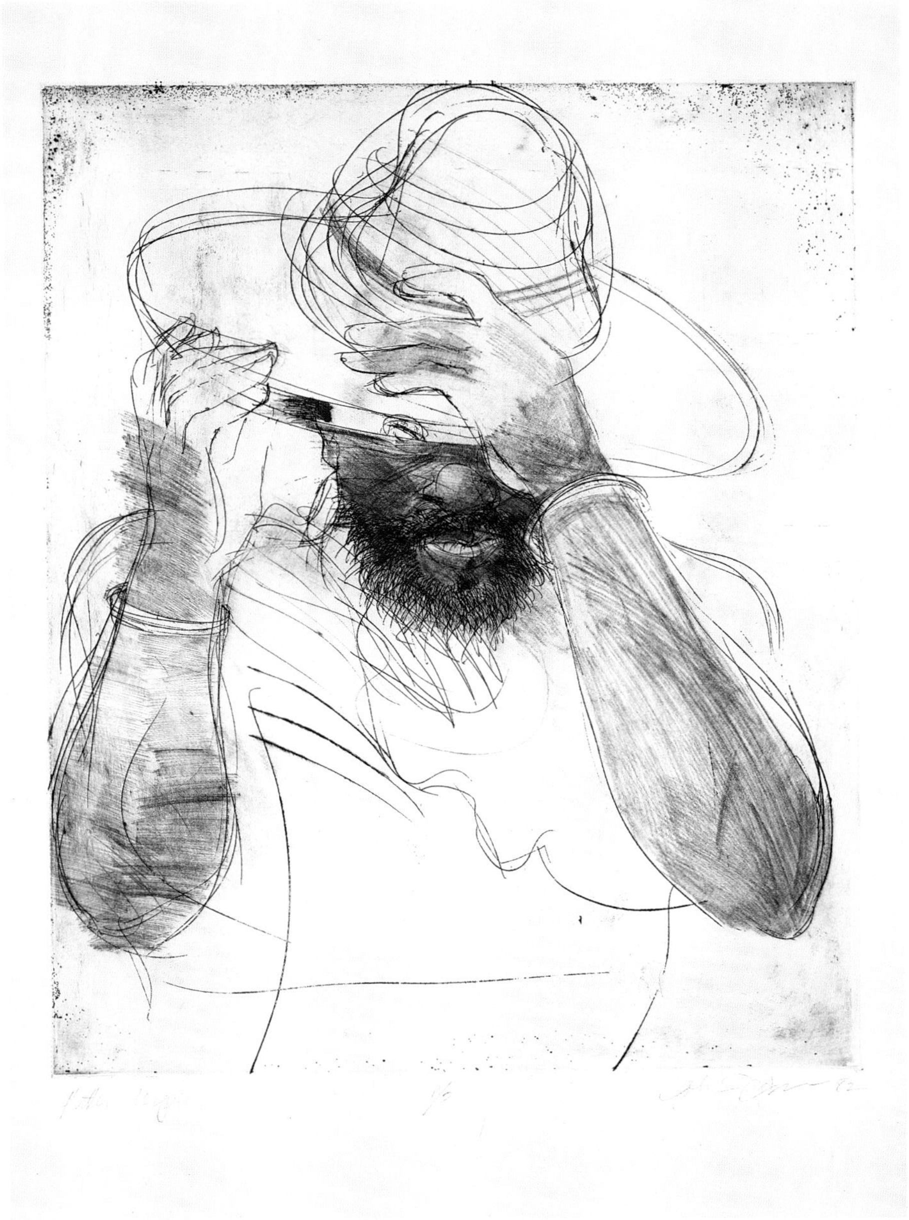

Hattin' Up, 1982. Intaglio, 19½" x 23½"

DIANE NEWTON Who doesn't remember the sweet satisfaction of a thick, clean, unused Big Chief tablet on the first day of school? Who cannot recall the smells of wax crayons and chalk, paste, tempera paint and cedar pencil shavings? And who has forgotten the satin smoothness of unchewed pencils and the gritty feel of a new parallelogram-shaped hard rubber eraser?

You can forget a lot, but not these things. The touch and aroma of paper, paint and graphite come to us early and hang around all our lives. Especially with artists.

Diane Newton will never forget the art set her parents gave her when she was very young. It was a magnificent gift filled with sheets of drawing paper and other artist's materials. The paper was thick and oatmeal colored with random flecks of wood fiber. There were charcoal sticks and a block of sandpaper to sharpen them, and a book of illustrations on how to draw. The author of the book gave art lessons on a syndicated television series. The instructions were based on the concept of identification of simple shapes and their use in the construction of more complex images.

Even after years of undergraduate and graduate studies in painting, the concept still makes sense to Diane Newton. No matter that it came from a television art teacher's lesson plan. Logic is important in her life, and it seems sensible to retain things that work well.

Today she lives in a large, pleasant house on a big lot in a neighborhood called Sleepy Hollow. The house sits deep back into the yard and the trees and a large amount of shrubbery almost hide it from the street. The interior is quiet and hospitable. The paintings on the wall, the books, the furnishings, the unstudied casualness of everything about the house reflects a warm and sincere lifestyle.

As we sit and talk in a large parlor area with sun splattering in through high windows, she demonstrates a cultivated intelligence, a broad range of potential to be almost anything she might choose to be. She is interested in language, in history, in travel and other cultures. She speaks knowledgeably and with confidence about a lot of things. And she doesn't show the least discomfiture when the baby wakes, the phone rings and someone arrives at the front door—all at the same time.

She clearly has the ability to do anything she wants with her life. But Diane Newton long ago cast her lot with painting. Now, after years of study, of intensive experimentation and development, she has reached the level of a resourceful, determined and highly skilled painter. She knows herself and what she is about. She works in bold, swift, impetuous strokes, anxious and impatient to see how the work will turn out. She cannot, or will not, wait on paint to dry or for an image to be transferred from printing plate to printing paper so she works in pastels—the most direct color medium available to an artist.

Diane uses pastel sticks with the familiarity gained from working for years and years with charcoal. The technique is the same: Use the end of the pastel, draw with it; turn it on its side for big, broad strokes; rub it; remove it; pile it on; smooth it out. The end result is different from charcoal, of course. Clear, clean color glows from the paper, a painting in every sense of the word—filled with rich nuances of color, texture, form and light.

At one time she experimented seriously with abstract concepts. Now she finds and organizes shape and form in landscape and figurative situations with the same sense of discipline and balance. Then she lights them up with passionate messages about life and people and places. It just seems sensible to retain things that work.

Mass Pike: June Rain, 1985. Pastel drawing, 30" x 44"

She works in bold, swift, impetuous strokes, anxious and impatient to see how the work will turn out. She cannot, or will not, wait on paint to dry.

FRANK NICHOLS I wasn't surprised when Frank Nichols told me he was a middle line backer on his high school football team. He has a low center of gravity, bulging biceps and a barrel chest and looks tough, strong and agile enough to still play that position. Put a ball cap and a gray sweatshirt on him, hang a whistle around his neck, and you have everyone's idea of what a coach should look like. And Frank Nichols does coach. Not lineman or backs or receivers, but earnest young men and women who come to him to learn the demanding disciplines of the printmaker's craft.

When Frank was growing up, it appeared that he was interested only in football, girls and the other preoccupations of boys his age in a small town on the Oklahoma line. Now after 30 years or so, he can talk about what was really going on inside of him during those years in Arkansas City. "I always knew there was another part of me waiting to get out," he confided. "I drew portraits of my friends and thought about writing poems and stories. I even tried to write a novel." He developed a passion for the epic sounds of classical music. All these things were present and growing stronger during the early rites of passage.

When it was time, he put everything together and began his journey into the misty landscapes of his subconscious. He began to add sum and substance to his own personal manifesto as an artist. In all that he did, he searched and struggled for meaning, tantalized by the nearness of new levels of reality.

As an artist should, he began to scrape away anything that dulled his perceptions, and in the process of learning to see and think like an artist, he discovered himself among a clutter of possibilities of what might have been.

Today, there is nothing in the world that he would rather be doing than working with students—preparing them, polishing them, pushing them to achieve their potential. In the time left over, there is nothing else that provides him more fulfillment than pouring out his feelings and ideas about reality onto richly burnished, almost sensual copper plates.

Nichols works freely, etching flowing linear images directly into the metal. Then he models light and dark patterns into the plate, often creating spatial ambiguities, adding to the mystery and the mood. Finally, he adds layer after layer of transparent watercolor pigment suspended in a clear acrylic medium which is brushed on in glazes. The effect is a beguiling hybrid of print texture and the spontaneity of paint.

The fact that the use of acrylic creates additional stability and long life for the print/paintings is important to Nichols. He is interested in making contributions that will survive deep into the future. He is convinced that artists can have a

special voice in developing an expanded human spirit through their special ability to reveal truth and reality.

Frank Nichols is almost a missionary in his zeal to encourage artists to pursue their own development and destiny through lifelong dedication to their own ideals. "No matter how long you live," he says,"time is too short to waste it on any other kind of serious diversion besides working and thinking and storing up experiences that will someday have something to do with your work."

Even so, Nichols pays a tough price in order to share his time as an artist with his time as a teacher. He sleeps an average of five hours a night, and his working hours are filled with a mixture of fast-moving chores. In his studio working places, both at home and on the campus, he is starting a plate, proofing one, painting another, or matting still another for some kind of showing.

In his studio-classrooms, he is engrossed in carrying out carefully thought out strategies for helping students move forward. The rewards of witnessing and being a part of their growth, he says, are something he can't put a price tag on. He shows me the work of one of his students who recently sold several hundred dollars worth of prints at an art fair in Kansas City. "More than I sold," he grins. The young woman's work is a skillfully and sensitively done tableaux of dancing wood nymphs. Nichols believes that she has "somehow tapped into a universal stream of innocence and goodness. It's a look that comes through in her work and people like it."

Even though his own work often does not sell as well, he is not disappointed. He's content to let the future be the judge of what he is doing now. "Besides," he says, "when one of my students does well, I know that my contribution helped make it happen. I can't lose. I can't wait to get out of bed every morning and get started. I guess I'm just about the luckiest man in the world."

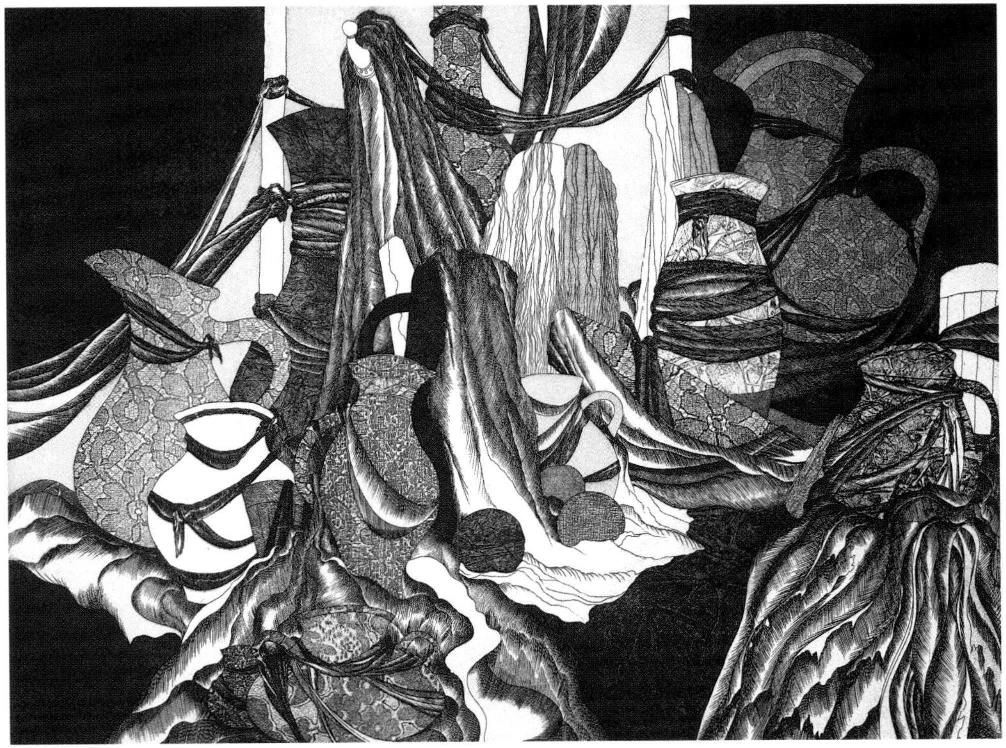

"No matter how long you live, time is too short to waste it on any other kind of serious diversion besides working and thinking..."

Community Still Life. Etching, 24" x 18"

Bea Opelka The setting for Bea Opelka's studio is reminiscent of some old illustrations I remember in *Hansel and Gretel.* There is a cottage in a forest and a studio peeking out from behind. The place is surrounded by that kind of suspended hushed quietness which I always feel on autumn days when the last surviving leaves come drifting down, one at a time, and a whisper of smoke floats off into the trees.

The studio is small with a loft-like arrangement. There are several large framed canvas paintings hanging around the main floor studio area. Aside from this, there is no evidence of work in progress. No paint on the floor; no open bottles of varnish, oil or thinner. No half-squeezed capless tubes. No piles of rags or randomly posted sketches, doodles or drawings. But for all of this antiseptic orderliness, the studio is warm with artistic presence. A stereo is playing chamber music. A light snack of cheese and fruit is laid out on white plastic dishes imprinted with quaint, old-fashioned blue wild flowers. To me, it feels like an artist's studio should feel.

During the war, Opelka's father, an attorney in Lithuania, sent Bea and her sister to live on their grandparent's farm in the northern part of their country. Bea's eyes look beyond the studio walls as she recalls the sunny days when she and her sister wandered through orchards in bloom, skipped underneath the silver blue boughs of great spruce trees and paused to pick bright cornflowers popping out of thick green fields of rye.

She remembers, too, the Lithuanian songs, poems and legends which unreservedly celebrate nature. Today, she acknowledges that her strong personal attachment to landscape paintings began with her earliest memories of the wonders of wind and earth and sky.

When she speaks of nature, there is an undercurrent of excitement in her voice. It is the largeness, the purity and the innocence of nature that attracts her attention and fires her imagination. It is, she says, her escape from the artificiality of manmade environments.

Opelka's paintings are the best evidence of a brilliant sense of unity between painter and the painting subject. Ranging up to several feet in width and length, they appear at first to be very matter-of-fact, quite literal oil paintings executed in a traditionally academic style. After a longer look, close and very subtle color relationships reveal themselves. Ochre and umber and other earth colors gain intensity and energy from pinks and blues and lavenders. Some of the relationships are so close together that they skirt on the edge of redundancy, but it all fits together in a quilt of larger patches of warm, colorful grays.

The textural relationships work well to create an atmospheric illusion of grass and wood, earth and sky—a mixture of soft and hard, of smooth and abrasive, of wet and dry. It comes to my mind that Bea Opelka is a magician—a mas-

ter illusionist—who can take you into a landscape, make you feel it, make you feel at home in it.

Her sorcery is never more evident than in her ability to create a warm feeling of intimacy and an enormous impression of unfilled space, all on the same canvas. Bea Opelka reaches out and embraces her landscape subjects.

"The landscape appears real and timeless to me," she says. "I am fascinated by its earthiness. Mud, dirt, weeds and grasses are unpretentious, yet infinitely beautiful. I am intrigued by wind, movements of clouds, fog and the smell of rain. When all else is in turmoil, there is a peacefulness out there that helps put everything into perspective."

During her progress to artistic maturity, she has worked in many mediums, experimented with abstract expressionism and moved through assorted other trends.

Now, she is home, translating space and feeling and a new dimension of artistic reality into the landscape—an art form that is replenished every time the sun comes up.

Flint Hills. Oil on canvas, 50" x 54"

Michael Ott When Michael Ott smiles, he looks like Ozzie Nelson. There is the same clear-eyed innocence. The same openness. The same refreshing directness. Michael Ott's voice, like Ozzie's, is pleasant to hear. When he speaks, the words come tumbling out, tinged with enthusiasm, slightly edged with excitement, and the message gains a sort of inner luminosity from the force of his sincerity. He wears sneakers, cords and a workshirt with the uncommon grace of a young stockbroker on his day off. Like Ozzie, here is a man you can trust to return your lawn mower.

Beyond the image, however, there is a strong and serious man with a deep and purposeful interest in matters of art and life. Sitting around the big oak table in the neat house on the inside fringe of the Kansas University campus seems natural and right for him. He appears to be interested in everything, and he gives the impression of being able to devour everything he sees and hears in huge, indiscriminate chunks.

There is a thirsty, carnivorous quality to Ott's pursuit of the truth of his times. There is so much happening, he says, that he could never be without some idea to explore with his painting. He absorbs so much and is touched by so much that he simply can see no end to it.

As a child, Ott didn't have art lessons, in or out of school, but he drew in a natural, confident style. As a Regents Scholar at Colorado University, he majored in math. And then architecture. And then, finally, when it became clear to him that he could major in art and keep his scholarship, he made the leap.

He went on to Berkeley for graduate study and then back to Kansas to teach. Today, the expansive watercolors he paints of empty shirts have grown out of his need to express some very specific things about his time and place in history.

The empty garments evoke a kind of intimate echo of what has been in a way that adds another dimension of understanding for those who will see the paintings beyond his time. He says he hopes for the same reaction from his audience as he gets when he sees the tiny articles of clothing his own children have outgrown.

His lectures on the language of clothing center around the fact that people wear what they do for functional reasons, for status and to identify themselves. Of these three reasons, he says status is probably the most important, though he is noticeably disturbed himself by pretense and snobbery.

His paintings are expertly executed in a challenging medium. Their messages are sensitive, poetic and clearly very personal. They speak out like a trip to the attic, a rummage through an old trunk, or the rediscovery of a toy from childhood.

There are strong undertones of other feelings in his work. The sadness of his mother's long illness. The loneliness of the flat, dusty fields south of Wichita where he grew up. The frustration he sometimes feels about the inequities of the art world.

But for all of this, Michael Ott is a contented man. Most of his time is spent either teaching, talking about, or making art. Sometimes in the midst of busy class schedules, studio chores and occasional babysitting, he dreams of doing nothing but painting for all of his waking hours. He once worked for several weeks in the distraction-free environment of a center for creative artists. There were no telephones to answer, he recalls, no errands to run, no interruptions of any kind. "It was strange," he said. "I don't know what that would be like on a permanent basis, but it would be fun to try."

Growing Family, 1986. Watercolor, 30" x 23"

His paintings speak out like a trip to the attic, a rummage through an old trunk, or the rediscovery of a toy from childhood.

MARY F. PALFFY There is a strange, haunting presence in the portrait of a cow which hangs in Mary Palffy's living room. This heifer from a herd of Brahmans crossed with Herefords is not standing in the traditional four-footed pose of prize cattle but is cropped down to the head and shoulder composition favored for humans. The one eye shown in the profile seems to be unaccountably wise and sensitive. There is a strong implication in the painting that the cow is a great deal more intelligent than is customarily believed.

The cross-breeding of Brahman and Hereford, Mary Palffy tells me, produces a very unusual animal. Her husband, David Patterson, who is completing a doctorate in animal physiology, is carrying out research required for the degree with a herd of 300 "Bra-ford" heifers somewhere in the Flint Hills. "When we walk into the pen," Palffy says, "the heifers are instantly aware and unusually alert. There is a look in their eyes like a light escaping from out of the dark."

The massive, heavy forms of the cow in the painting seem almost buoyant, supported in space by invisible wires and pylons. She has the ability and the training to add the discipline of architecture to her painting and printmaking. She thinks in terms of weights and balances, the harmonious distribution of space, and the continuation of the image. All the while, she also thinks in the curiously enigmatic, fanciful way of a poet.

In her search for a precise image, Mary Palffy journeys through layer after layer of emotion, experience and feeling. For years now, she has experimented with themes involving sheep and cattle. In some works, they appear to step out of nowhere to stand silently in the pastures of dream landscapes. In others, the realism of the animals must be found through abstractions. Whatever they are and whatever their purpose, the works are powerful and provocative. They are clearly done to cause people to think, feel and listen to their own inner voices.

The use of figural elements of cattle and sheep in Palffy's work may have been predestined. She grew up in Bozeman, Montana, a town surrounded on all sides by great sprawling ranch lands. Her mother descended from a family that had settled in the area in 1863, even before it had gained territorial status. Her father, a Hungarian emigre, became a Montana cowboy after serving as a tailor, a soldier and a merchant seaman. Her husband grew up in a Montana ranching family also. Cattle ranching and agrarian influences have always been strong in her life and now they are more than distant echos in her work. She describes what she does as building blocks that will inevitably lead somewhere else.

Palffy is a handsome, vigorous woman with a contagious sense of adventure about her. She was born in the Russian sector of Vienna during the Cold War year of 1953. At the same time, the woman who was to become her adoptive mother was on her way to Europe to enjoy a heavy schedule of opera. As the woman began her trip, her husband casually commented that perhaps she should bring home a refugee baby. (The Palffys were childless and beyond the age of eligibility to adopt in the United States).

In Vienna, an infant was found and the adoption process was begun, an ordeal involving completion of adoption papers, stacks of affidavits and endless interviews. Mary's mother persevered, stealing time with the baby during the day and losing herself in majestic high-arching music every night at the opera and finally, after six months, the adoption was completed. Mary Palffy came home to Bozeman with her mother. Mary has warm and tender memories about growing up with the help of two wise and understanding parents.

When she was a junior in high school, her father died and one year later, her mother was gone, too. By Palffy's account, they were "unique in their ability to pursue all of life's opportunities to the fullest measure," a legacy that Mary Palffy treasures.

Leathermaker V, 1986. Intaglio, mixed media and lithography, $29\frac{9}{16}$" x $41\frac{1}{2}$"

DEBORAH SCHLIER The road to Dallas is wide and open and fast. If you get started early from Wichita, you'll get there in time for the six o-clock news. On the way, you'll be entertained by the view of hills and valleys and fields and towns sliding by. Turn on the right music, set the cruise control and it's like being in a 3-D movie; life imitating art.

Shortly after Christmas, Debbie Schlier rented a U-haul trailer, sorted through her books and her clothing and her artist's things and headed down that road to Dallas. This symbolic step into full, free-standing, non-student adulthood was not a tough one for her to take. Getting a graduate degree and then finding a teaching job had always been the plan. Now she was on her way. In a sense, it was a homecoming. She was born in Amarillo and she would share a small apartment with her sister, a Dallas banker.

In Debbie's case, growing up meant learning to do your best and accepting the outcome without complaint. She enjoyed a nurturing childhood. She grew up with the understanding that effort is ultimately the resource for all worthwhile rewards. During this time, she happily colored and drew and made paper constructions and sewed. Art and craft projects of all kinds were the intriguing, challenging moments in her life, the times when she felt most in control, most able, most worthy.

Becoming an artist seemed a natural for Debbie for hers is an unwavering commitment to the search for creative insight and innocence. Her efforts towards this goal are clearly expressed in bold, clean color and daringly innovative compositions. She leaps the fences of conventionality to do what she must do and to say what she wants to say. And she does it with both vigor and aplomb.

The types of things she does are brilliantly amusing and possess strong decorative appeal but her work, she insists, is more than an interesting surface-graphic. There is a heavy message—an underlying psychological or sociological meaning in what she does. She expects her work to move those who see it, to create feelings in them that they would not otherwise experience.

She works through a startling range of media and media combinations: Woodcuts, intaglios, graphite drawings, serigraphs on homemade paper, collages, multimedia monotypes, latex and ink on canvas, oil and acrylic paintings, watercolors. All are handled deftly and unceremoniously.

Working with new combinations of materials, she believes, adds an extra creative dimension, and extends the potential for new discovery. The apartment where she lives with her sister and her niece is too small to accommodate on-purpose studio quarters, so until they can move into a larger place, she paints in her bedroom. She misses printmaking and the room to continue unrestricted experimentation with an array of media combinations. Collage, she thinks, makes the best use of her limited studio facilities.

The fresh contemporary look of her work has persuaded the large art and antique Dallas gallery where she is now employed as a framer/designer to represent her. The work she is doing is interesting and educational. She is learning the ways of the very rich and absorbing the special cultural opportunities now available to her. She has overcome the shock of the move to a large, fast-moving metropolitan area and feels comfortable with the big city tempo.

She still plans to be an artist who teaches, and the prospects are picking up. She has had several requests for her resume from colleagues, and at last year's College Art Association meeting in Houston, she was singled out with a dozen others from a field of hundreds to be interviewed for one of the most prestigious art schools in the nation. She didn't get the job but, she says, "the honor of just being interviewed was a terrific boost." Debbie Schlier believes in the future. And that's the very best reason for being an artist.

Stone Cake, 1985. Intaglio, 9" x 12"

Kathleen Shanahan Like artists everywhere, Kathleen Shanahan carries around a storehouse in her head. She gathers images with the vigilance of a sharp-eyed bird; finding small treasures wherever she travels, wherever she looks. The sparkle of sweat on the brow of a celebrant in a Japanese ritual; the way the Aegean Sea looks in the moonlight; the shadowy silhouettes along French canal banks at night; the clear amber of tea being poured. It's all put away, all creative inventory.

Her grandmother's large, mid-Victorian house remains especially sharp and clear in Kathleen Shanahan's memory. Its angular shapes and vertical thrusts sharply punctuated its resemblance to a castle. Its porches and bay windows and railings and buttresses were heavily accented by ornamental mill work—the stuff architects call gingerbread, the stuff house painters call a nightmare.

The overly decorated exterior was carried on inside the house. It was stuffed with collections of dolls and clusters of framed photographs and prints and multiple doilies on the arms and seats and backs of chairs and sofas and scatter rugs and vases and figurines and crystal and china and books and odds and bits of memorabilia of every kind.

The effect of it all was a dense and mysterious look, the same sort of feeling that comes from an artist's collage. Experiences and memories are layered, each partly on top of the other; submerged until they filter back to the surface, magically and forever changed into artful expression.

Collage shows up frequently in the images Kathleen Shanahan makes. Small, cut-out overlays of paper and tinsel affixed on large acrylic paintings of Japanese ceremonials deepen the sense of sharing an older experience, an intimacy, a closeness, a feeling of having been a part of it all before. Like opening an old trunk stored in an attic. Or going through a long forgotten family photo album.

The images have been put away for several years. They were accumulated when she went to Japan as a visiting scholar at the National Museum of Ethnology in Osaka. In the 14 months she spent there, she immersed herself in the curious mixtures of ancient rituals and contemporary western culture. She made sketches and traveled into the countryside. She deferred painting for making notes, gathering ideas and thoughts for future development. Now it's all coming out.

When I came around the corner of the Ulrich Museum Gallery where her part of the Wichita State faculty show was hung, there were no people but I sensed a cloud of voices, rising from the paintings like the clear call of unseen geese on a distant horizon.

In my imagination, the large panels functioned like a cinema. Bittersweet recollections of *Teahouse of the August Moon* rolled film frames through my mind and other Japanese images from other films flickered across my memory.

Kathleen Shanahan paints like a powerful soprano sings. Bright bold images flow around each other in a stream of pure feeling. She has the means to dig beneath the surface and to layer what she finds there into a deep and abiding emotional encounter.

She works in acrylic on medium-sized panels. Pastel is sometimes substituted for paint. And she uses other media like graphite and prism pencils, ink and airbrush. She draws with great power and confidence, a validation of her serious study of sculpture. The result is a realism combined with a highly evocative style that suggests even more than it shows.

She is physically small and, like her indomitable grandmother who cherished independence of thought and action into her nineties, Kathleen Shanahan follows her intuition, her inner signals. In her work, in her intellect, in her adventurous spirit, she towers over her diminutive size. One of her Japanese colleagues once told a countryman that Kathleen was a fine artist, even though she didn't look like one. That's true.

The first time I met Kathleen Shanahan was in her office. She looked small and vulnerable. Ziggy, her Scottie, shuffled out from under a chair to look me over. His eyes were beady and black and he resembled a dog in a children's book who smokes a pipe and wears a battered straw hat. I could see him playing a kind of Toto to her Dorothy, two elfish spirits bounding down a yellow brick road. And I can see them now, off to see the Wizard.

Rites Oblike/Moving Walk: The Hod Carrier, 1985. Acrylic gold leaf and collage on Masonite, 2' x 8'

GORDON SHERMAN It is half past seven and already cold and dark when I set out to look for Gordon Sherman's house. I find it in one of the working class neighborhoods that wrap around the city's tired old downtown area. The streets are empty and only a few lights show through the windows up and down the block. There is a lost and lonely cast to the place. It is too quiet. Windblown leaves skitter down the frozen sidewalk—running away like a pack of small animals.

Gordon Sherman is watching for me from the front window. He is a tall, red-bearded man wearing striped overalls and heavy working man's shoes. I follow him to a dining alcove where we take our places across from one another at a very large, darkly stained table. The furnishings are old and ill-matched and undersized light bulbs do nothing more than create dim puddles of light.

The rooms all seem to run together. Aside from the incongruous presence of original avant garde paintings, drawings and prints hanging on the walls, the home seems entirely functional: a place to go away from in the morning and return to at night.

But it's all right for Gordon Sherman. Although he has two college degrees and considerable professional recognition as a painter and printmaker, he makes his living as a construction carpenter. And this is a construction worker's house. Every working day, Gordon puts on heavy, rough clothing, picks up his hard hat and lunch bucket and enters a world where everything is dealt with in stark black and white, right and wrong; it either works or it doesn't. It is a world where people trade muscle and sweat for wages. Nails are driven. Lumber is cut. Loads are lifted. Structures are raised. Energy pours out—and sometimes at the end of a day there is nothing left over.

But it is a good trade-out as far as Gordon Sherman is concerned, at least for right now. Somehow he can always find enough strength to paint. And he is proud that he and he alone decides what he paints and how he paints it. He is the classic, struggling artist. And he loves it all: the smell of the paint, the images forming on canvas and paper, the idea of creating.

It's all worth what you have to pay, he thinks. Even the pain and disappointment have a value. They make you more sharply aware of creative opportunities, he says, and keep you on your toes. Gordon is suspicious of being too comfortable. If he has any deep concerns, it's that the part of the price his wife and two children must pay might be too much. But it's their struggle, too, and they are eager to help.

Sometimes when Gordon is too tired to do anything but sit silently, letting the warmth and strength seep back into his body, his little boy comes to him and

asks that they go to the studio, a made-over storage shed in back of the house. "He knows what's going on and he wants to help," Gordon says. "My whole family is my inspiration. They keep me going."

Gordon Sherman's art is wildly mystical. Strange figures with twisted parts emerge from shadowy backgrounds. Bound and helmeted figures with no trace of their origin, no reasonable purpose for their existence, appear out of the mists of his imagination. The colors, shapes, forms and situation are totally of his own invention. Sometimes the images seem to have a life of their own, coming from somewhere outside his conscious memory or motivation.

Outside of a possible opportunity to sell some illustrations, Sherman sees nothing greatly different for himself or his family in the future. "It's too late now to sell out," he resolutely shakes his head. "My kids like it that they are the only ones at school who can say that they have an artist for a father. That's something."

Find A Foreign Place, 1986. Oil on canvas, 72" x 48"

Bound and helmeted figures with no trace of their origin, no reasonable purpose for their existence, appear out of the mists of his imagination.

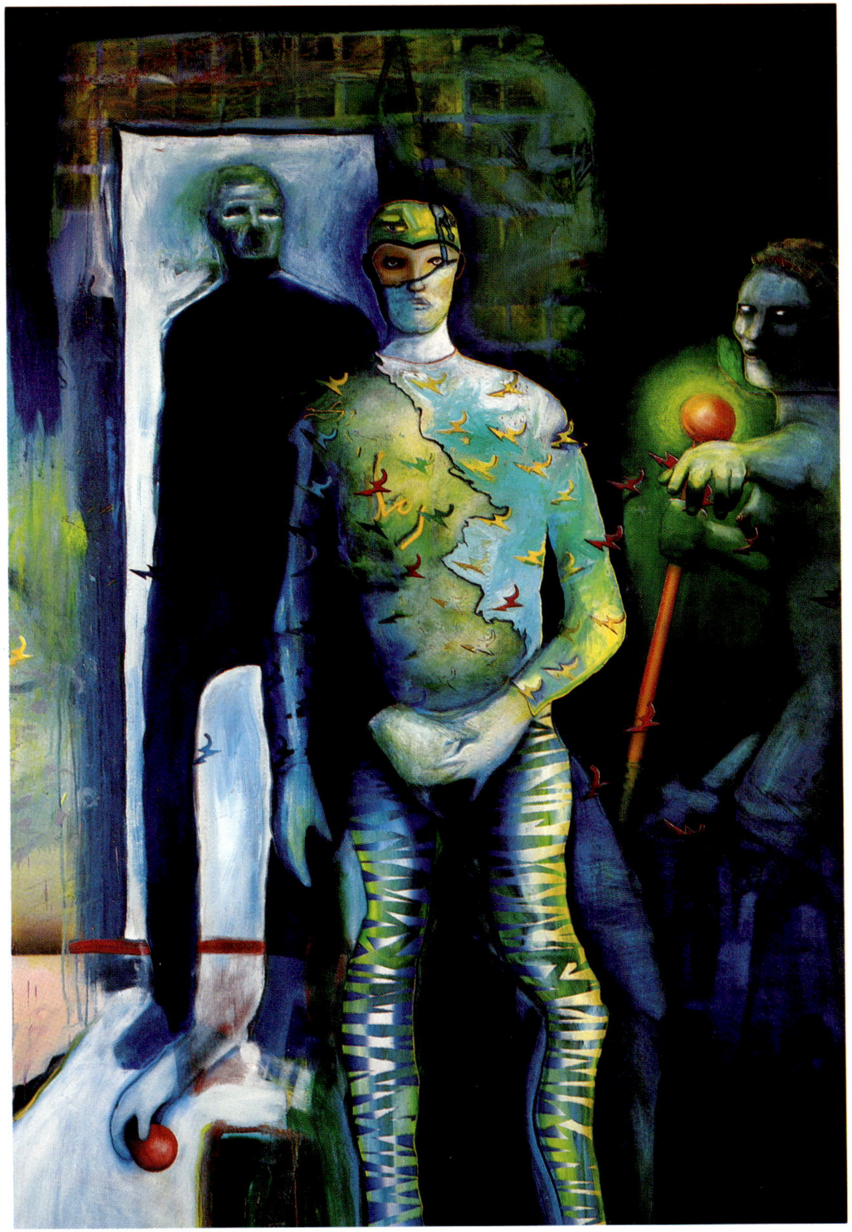

ROGER SHIMOMURA I met Roger Shimomura on a Sunday morning. On the way to his house I drove by a small church with weather-stained clapboard siding. It was a gray day in autumn and an old black woman entering the church with bright artificial flowers in her hat reminded me of how wonderful color can make you feel.

Shimomura lives south of 9th on Connecticut Street on the east side of Lawrence. It is a poor section of town, made up mostly of old, nondescript houses of many sizes and shapes. It is a place where broken fences and sagging gates are ordinary sights and neatly trimmed lawns with freshly painted shutters are rarely seen. Part of the area has been taken over by a railroad siding and small warehouses, plants and workshops.

From the outside, Shimomura's house fits into the area. The inside, however, has been gutted and converted into a very large studio with screens and easels, desks and work areas scattered with artistic casualness throughout the sunlit interior. The furniture and household accessories are clean-lined and functional. There is a contemporary look and feel to the proportions and placement of things about the room. Although it could be either Scandinavian or Oriental, the style is actually Japanese-American—a distinctive identity made up of influences from both, but in sum total is different from either.

Shimomura is sharply conscious of the distinction. When he was three years old, his family, along with thousands of other Japanese, were exiled to a dreary, dusty detention camp in a remote part of Idaho. They had lived in Seattle where his father was a pharmacist. In time, they made their way back to the Pacific Northwest, but the memories of the camp are still with them.

Shimomura's father wanted him to be a physician, but he chose graphic design instead. Years of producing both designs and finished production art gave him an easy virtuosity in his drawing skills and in his understanding of artist's materials and techniques. During that particular part of his career, Shimomura worked on everything from neon signs to menus to costume illustration.

At one point, he was given the responsibility for the design of the Polynesian Pavilion at the New York World's Fair. It was a success of a kind, but the thought of doing things that had nothing at all to do with pleasing clients kept popping into his head. Memories of things he had been told in college art classes became clear, coherent and logical. He began to explore the possibilities of becoming a painter.

He began with a formal study program which consumed years of undergraduate and graduate work. In graduate school, he became totally absorbed

with Pop Art, Andy Warhol and the funk art movement emerging on the West Coast. By the early 70s he was established in Lawrence and his work had turned to an Asian context. He did a series of 25 paintings, all representing entries from his grandmother's diary. They are sad, poignant and remonstrative statements speaking out in the same kind of voice as might a Daumier or a Hogarth. Many people understand the paintings very well, he observes, because there is no single answer intended.

A large painting in one corner of the studio incorporates pop images of Donald Duck, Pinocchio, Samarai figures, Kabuki dancers and a self-portrait. "Some might see it as a big party," he sighs. "Others may go far beyond that to learn more about themselves."

Shimomura cuts a handsome, theatrical figure and speaks in an actor's voice. He shares his time as a painter with his passion for writing, directing and producing plays that employ nontraditional means and techniques. These theatrical performances involve a six or seven member ensemble of dancers and actors who perform in ballrooms and recital halls, as well as in art galleries.

His newest play will require a full 45-foot stage. When he's writing his performance art adventures, he feels the presence of new ideas for painting. Then when he returns to painting, he discovers ideas for a performance arts production. For all of his 20-year sojourn in Kansas, there are elements of the traditional Oriental theater in his plays and Japanese imagery in his paintings. Of his two cultural heritages, he is quick to say that he is neither one or the other but both, a distillation of Japanese-American thought and history. "There are no reasons why we should have any special skill in the use of chopsticks," he says, "even though we have a special affinity to the tradition."

Shimomura is a prodigious worker with a staggering amount of output. Column after column of entries on his resume describe his awards, honors, exhibitions and publication references, but he measures success from several points of view. Of the 25 paintings in the Grandmother's Diary Series, only four were left unsold. All include barbed wire. It's important, he thinks, that they be sold, too.

Untitled, 1986. Acrylic on canvas, 60" x 72"

Richard Thomas Siegman Tom Siegman and I sit in a large reception area in the Senior Service Center and talk while another meeting is going on in a far corner of the room. The center is located in an old red factory building at the east end of a bridge that crosses the Arkansas River. As we talk we can hear traffic whizzing by and the melodic voice of a young lady conducting a meeting of senior citizens. Every once in a while, there is a burst of laughter.

Tom, who is not yet 40, is working under a private grant which calls for him to serve part-time as an art teacher at the Senior Services Center. The other half of his time, the grant stipulates, is to be spent developing his art.

In regard to the type of art work he does, he identifies himself as a "drawer," very carefully accenting each syllable to let you know that he knows it is not the right word. He is serious that this is the best way to describe what he is and what he does. He makes prints and paints and creates special kinds of photographic images. "Around here," he grins, "people ask me if I'm an oil painter, and I tell them I am, but I have also been known to paint with latex, enamel and asphalt."

Tom uses anything that's around and available to express and put down the private images that float to the top of his creative memory. There is about him the romanticism of a real artist, the kind for whom art is life.

An only child, his earliest recollections are of drawing pictures and being praised for it. After high school he tried college, dropped out, joined the Navy, tried college once more and quit again. Eventually, he found the right school, finished and came to Wichita State University for graduate work.

We move out of the main building and walk cautiously through the dark across a gravel parking area to a smaller structure where Tom teaches men and women old enough to be his grandparents. It is well lighted, reasonably neat and clean and equipped with a hodge-podge of drawing desks, tables, chairs and some very flimsy easels. Nothing quite matches. It looks as if it has been hastily assembled and made available for people who would not have the background to be too critical.

On the way to the corner which Tom claims as his own, we pass by some unfinished student work. It has a neat, sincere, somewhat overworked look, the trademark of those who have not done it long enough to make it look easy, natural and sophisticated.

I sit in a folding metal chair and look at some of Tom's work. Tom is languid, tall and thin. He moves slowly and with careful concentration on what he is doing and saying. The work he shows me has a very deep, resonant quality, full of echoes. It's like looking into a deep well full of shadows and calling out a loud hello.

The silver print photos, in particular, make me strain to think about what it is there that makes them so special to me. Try as I will, I cannot. I am convinced that his photographic print of a little black girl holding a fish by its tail and smiling into the camera is more than the sum of its parts.

Tom is driven more by poetic intuition than by his craftsmanship. He is inclined to move into the process of making a piece of art with the expectation of finding inspiration through encounters with accidents that are certain to happen along the way. He doesn't think of himself as a person teaching elderly people in a hobby shop setting. "I teach just like I would teach in a university setting," he says. "I only know how to teach one way. I don't know what the hell art therapy is."

The thing that excites Tom Siegman most about being an artist is to look at his own work after it's done. He is always surprised at what comes out of himself through his work. "Even when I work from a figure model, I'm looking for what's really going on, inventing ways to describe what's going on. Everything that I know somehow seems to wind up there."

Slow Pitch, 1984. Drawing, 30" x 22"

The work has a very deep, resonant quality, full of echoes. It's like looking into a deep well full of shadows and calling out a loud hello.

ROBERT SUDLOW I remember watching four-engine seaplanes roar off to hunt submarines during World War II. They would rise ponderously from the sea like winged whales shedding water from their bellies. In a short time, they would be gone, leaving behind only the distant mournful sounds of their engines.

Bob Sudlow is the only person I have met since the war who flew those great lumbering patrol bombers. Day after day, he sat on the flight deck of his PBM flying boat looking down, taking in miles of the Pacific in one sweeping glance after another. To a young aviator from Kansas, the topography and moods of the ocean were similar to the rolling hills and pasture lands of home. Both provided the same unrestricted sense of freedom to see everything, and both invited the most extravagant visions.

Gazing out on the pitching waves and deep troughs and shifting shadows presented Sudlow with a restless panorama of color and texture, form and dynamic symmetry. It could have been here that he began in earnest to sort and think and feel his way through the incredible volume of visual experiences he was collecting. Mostly, these visions were of space, of huge caverns of sunlit air and great pile-ups of clouds and endless horizons.

Flying down the ocean coasts and out to sea stirred feelings in Sudlow that were later to find expression in the elemental masses and forms of sky and earth. The pieces were coming together. After the war, Sudlow never turned his attention to the sea again. Although he spent 20 summers on the California coast, he puts the ocean at his back and looks inland when he paints.

Over the years he has sought out high places where he could look out on large muscular land forms, spread out and falling away from where he worked. It is this unfolding, peeling away and opening up that

characterizes his work today. There is an omniscient quality to everything he paints, a sense of the heat, the cold, the wind, and all of the most intimate details of the time and place which he is telling you about.

He works spontaneously and intensely on large pieces of canvas. "I get so exalted, so carried away," he confides, "that often I feel I am painting beyond myself." He paints almost entirely in the out-of-doors. He attacks the canvas vigorously and abstractly, working quickly and thinly on toned canvas to catch the essence of something that may last less than half an hour. Sometimes, it's so cold he dresses in his old flight gear. When he has finished, he brings the results back to the studio where he can see it again, think about it and look for other ways to say what he wants to say. "When I return with a painting," he says, "I have air in my lungs and I have traveled a distance."

Wabaunsee Creek, 1987. Oil on canvas, 20" x 16"

To a young aviator from Kansas, the topography and moods of the ocean were similar to the rolling hills and pasture lands of home.

JACK WILSON The gray, concrete studios of the university art building are as impersonal as an empty laundromat spilling cold midnight light onto a deserted street. Even the drawings and prints taped to the walls are lost in the great blank look of the place, as if they were tiny flecks of colorful confetti, trailing off into pools of deep shadow.

When Jack Wilson walked in, the whole scene changed. It was like meeting an old friend in Grand Central Station when you're both alone and a long way from home. The space shrinks, the light mellows, and you're glad you're right where you are.

"Jack Wilson is a great guy, you'll like him," people had told me. And they were right. Jack Wilson is an enormously likeable young man. No one could be more honest, more open, more trusting. Ask him anything. And listen. His life, his art, his hopes and aspirations will come rippling by in a gentle stream of words.

Jack saunters on to the center stage of a conversation, claims the spotlight and brings with him an extra dimension of sharp, penetrating reality. But for all of this, there's nothing singularly spectacular about him. He is slightly built, dresses indifferently and does not invest in expensive haircuts. He is friendly, talkative and supremely confident and bears a sort of spiritual resemblance to Dobie Gillis and James Dean. In his own way, Jack Wilson reflects every man. He loves his home, his wife, his son, his work. He wants to make life mean something, to make a contribution to the common good. But when he was very young, the thought came to him that he was meant to do something special—and he has aggressively pursued ways to express whatever his individual destiny is supposed to be.

Even as early as the elementary grades, he fashioned alternative ways to do things. For him, it was never enough to walk straight down the middle of the path of accepted procedures, methodology and knowledge. In high school, his grades reflected a stubborn rejection of popular convention and consensus. In the great tradition, Jack Wilson was engaged in the making of an artist, inventing himself. As a college art student, he discovered the heady freedom to express himself without boundaries or restraints. He was encouraged by his teachers to explore as boldly and as recklessly as he pleased.

He celebrated the rite of graduation by converting all of his undergraduate canvas paintings into drop cloths. He met and married a kindred soul—a poet, painter, ceramist—who keeps a diary of her dreams and executes clear accounts of them in clay and other materials. They made a commitment to each other and each to their art. They both went back to school: Jack into printmaking, his wife into ceramics.

Jack found a half-way station between pure painting and pure printmaking. He continues to think like a painter while using the structure of the printmaking process to add control and discipline to his work. The results are often breathtaking in their sheer virtuosity and creative scope.

Jack mixes the printmaking medium with the romantic abandon of an abstract expressionist painter and the cool deliberation of a master printmaker. His work loses none of its spontaneity and passion in the translation. He capitalizes on things that happen in the printmaking process. A splash of solvent on a plate becomes a vital and effective part of the final image. And each print in an edition gains its own special identity through subtle changes in the actual printing.

His combinations of woodcuts, intaglios, lithographs and color reliefs are consciously of his own style and invention. There may be a hint of Tomayo in the intense oranges, vermillions and reds; or a suggestion of Rouault in the heavy, black drawing of the figures. But what you see is mostly what comes fresh from Jack Wilson's vivid imagination and from his passion to make art.

Since his earlier days, Jack has learned that the things he makes are worth saving, worth looking at, even worth money. He has a dealer. And friends. He doesn't roam around as much, or party as much. He is beginning to see some kind of future for himself. And it will involve art.

Drunken Escapade #3, 1986. Four block woodcut, 26½″ x 39½″

He continues to think like a painter while using the structure of the printmaking process to add control and discipline to his work.

Ranal Young The house where Ranal Young lives is not far from the center of the city but it looks like a cottage at the end of a country lane. It's made of manufactured logs and it has a front porch. It's the kind of house that goes with hollyhocks, a garden and petunia-filled flower boxes. It's a place that makes you remember things.

Trunks in attics with dusty light drifting through cracks in an abandoned barn. A box full of old letters, school papers and left-over unmatched Christmas wrappings. An Atwater Kent radio in a very large walnut veneer cabinet, one knob missing. Dolls with chipped faces, faded wedding pictures, a strip of gray-yellow lace, a bundle of old *National Geographics*, beads and pearls and shiny bits of jewelry spilling out of a dark-stained dresser drawer. A forgotten pair of shoes. An ancient post card. A campaign button. The aroma of cedar and bay rum and talcum powder.

Ranal Young's work reverberates with echoes: strong, persistent voices calling you home again. Listen, they say, to your mother's call to supper as it hangs out there on the darkening evening air. Or pay attention, the work insists, to the sound of a school bell, clanging softly, far off in your memory. Ranal Young has tapped into the world of submerged feelings and thoughts, experiences and memories.

In a unique and purposeful way, the assemblages follow the same process used in creating a painting. First there is an idea. Then a broadly defined mental image, then a first mark on the surface of the work. Afterwards, it becomes a matter of moving things about, exploring, experimenting, pulling and pushing and shaping the bits and pieces into relationships that work, that gain a coherency and a meaning beyond chaos.

But unlike two-dimensional painted images, the objects Ranal Young assembles in her work already exist, already have a history, already have a special reality of their own. The doll that someone else might create in a painting is actually a doll in her work. And the real doll projects not only a single image but multiple layers of thoughts and feelings of where it might have been and what it might have meant at other times to other people.

The work is openly theatrical, small stages set with ornate, jewel-like objects, woven together in tight tapestry-like designs. It's all very inventive and very hard to classify.

Ranal Young has an extensive background in painting and printmaking. She is a mature and respected professional in the world of serious makers of art. Her turn away from painting and into assemblage and mixed media was motivated by what she sees as an opportunity for fresh, more adventurous creative

explorations.

She deals with tiny universes of her own making, small worlds that expand into glittering fantasies, each with a life of its own. She looks upon assemblage like quilting as a lately liberated, serious art form. It doesn't matter to her that the idea of putting beads, cloth, stitchery, trinkets, toys, buttons and sundry other things usually found among needles and thread and sewing supplies can be identified as a hobby handcraft by those who don't know any better.

She knows the difference. She manipulates materials with a skill and understanding—and at an emotional depth—that transcends clever craftsmanship. Even the whimsical touches have great depth, substance and sophistication.

A mixed media presentation of a pearl-encrusted anchor with an ornate backdrop of more beads, pearls and embroidered cloth, showcases a tiny snapshot of a wistful voyager, sad and alone. At first glance, it reminded me of something to be found in an Eastern Orthodox Church. Then I could hear in my imagination a deep resonant rising of a big full sound, like an echo rushing out, breaking free.

Ranal Young's work can be powerful stuff; moody and strangely articulate. Her preoccupation with found objects and old things seems to fit her Southern heritage—old antebellum mansions, lace gowns, strings of pearls—and places and other things lost in time and space.

Log Cabin, 1983. Assemblage of mixed media, 21″ x 15½″ x 2″

First there is an idea. Then a broadly defined mental image, then a first mark on the surface of the work.

Biographies

JANE ASBURY — Page 4
Born 1943, New York, N.Y. —BFA, Indiana University, 1968; MFA, Indiana University, 1971. Exhibitions: *Midwest Printmakers Invitational*, N.E. Illinois University; *Regional Painting Invitational*, University of Nebraska; *Mid-Four*, Nelson-Atkins Museum, Kansas City, Mo. Represented in Collections: Rutgers State University,Camden, N.J., and Tulsa City County Library, Tulsa, Okla.

PHILOMENE BENNETT — Page 6
Born 1935, Lincoln, Neb. —BFA, University of Nebraska, 1956. Exhibitions: *National Women in Art,* Suzanne Brown Gallery, Scottsdale, Ariz.; *Kansas Collection,* National Museum of Women in the Arts, Washington, D.C.; *Summer Invitationals,* Nelson-Atkins Museum, Kansas City, Mo. Represented in Collections: Hallmark Collection, Kansas City, Mo.; Nelson-Atkins Museum, Kansas City, Mo.; National Museum of Women in the Arts, Washington, D.C.

DAVID BERNARD — Page 8
Born 1913, Sandwich, Ill. —BFA, University of Illinois, 1939; MFA, University of Iowa, 1949. Exhibitions: *Society of American Graphic Artists Exchange Exhibition to Japan; Collagraphs by David Bernard and Students of Wichita State University*, National Collection of Fine Arts (Discovery) Gallery, Smithsonian Institute, Washington. D.C. Represented in Collections: Library of Congress, Pennell Collection; The Metropolitan Museum of Art, N.Y., N.Y.; Otis Art Institute of L.A. County, Calif.

JOHN BOYD — Page 10
Born 1939, London, Ark. —BA, California State University at Long Beach, 1968; MFA, Cranbrook Academy of Art, Mich., 1971. Exhibitions: *Cimarron National Work on Paper,* Gardner Art Gallery, Oklahoma State University; *Boston Printmakers 41st North American Print Exhibition,* Emmanuel College, Boston, Mass.; *22nd Bradley National Print & Drawing Exhibition,* Bradley University, Peoria, Ill. Represented in Collections: Clemson University, S. C.; Texas Tech University, Lubbock, Texas; University of Wisconsin, Parkside, Kenosha, Wis.

VERNON BREJCHA — Page 12
Born 1942, Ellsworth, Kan. —MS, Fort Hays State University, Kan. 1967; MFA, University of Wisconsin, 1972. Exhibitions: *National Glass Invitational*, Louisville Art Gallery; *New Forms in Glass,* Horizon Gallery, Mill Valley, Calif.; *Tenth Anniversary Celebration*, Heller Galleries, N.Y., N.Y. Represented. in Collections: Smithsonian Institute; Kunstmuseum, Dusseldorf, West Germany; Moderne International Glaskunst Museum, Ebeltoft, Denmark

RONALD W. CHRIST — Page 16
Born 1949, St. Louis, Mo. —BFA, Kansas City Art Institute, Mo. 1972; MFA, Indiana University, 1974. Exhibitions: *The Amarillo Competition,* Amarillo, Tex.; *Director's Invitational*, Wichita Art Association, Wichita, Ks.; *Washington and Jefferson College National Painting Show*, Washington, Pa. Represented in Collections: United States Embassy, Colombo, Sri Lanka; University of Kansas School of Medicine-Wichita, Wichita, Kan.

JANE L. EBY — Page 14
Born 1954, Madison, Wis. —BFA, Midwestern State University, Texas, 1975; MFA, Wichita State University, Kan. 1979. Exhibitions: *Tenth Annual Southwestern Area Art Show*, Museum of the Southwest, Midland, Texas; *Connecticut College Print Invitational,* New London, Conn; *Mid-Four Annual Juried Exhibition*, Nelson-Atkins Museum, Kansas City, Mo. Represented in Collections: Wichita State University; Fort Hays State University, Fort Hays, Kan.; City of Salina, Salina, Kan.

DALE ELDRED — Page 22
Born 1934, Minneapolis, Minn. —BS, University of Michigan, 1957; MS, University of Michigan, 1959. Exhibitions: *Contemporary Arts Museum*, Houston, Texas; *Laumeier Sculpture Park*, with Christo and Michael Heizer, St. Louis, Mo.; *Citywide Contemporary Sculpture Exhibition*, Toledo, Ohio. Represented in Collections: The Metropolitan Museum of Art, N.Y.; Nelson-Atkins Museum of Art, Kansas City, Mo.; Hayden Gallery M.I.T., Cambridge, Mass.

JOAN FOTH — Page 26
Born 1930, Elmira, N.Y. —High School of Music & Art, N.Y., N.Y.; BA, Barnard College, N.Y., N.Y. Exhibitions: *Postcards for Association of Community Arts Agencies of Kansas,* 1980 and 1982; *Governor's Artist Award*; *Kansas Landscape Touring Exhibition*, Washington,. D.C. Represented in Collections: Wichita Art Museum, Wichita, Kan.; Hallmark Collection, Kansas City, Mo.; Vincent Price, Los Angeles, Calif.

BARBARA FRETS — Page 19
Born 1929, St. Louis, Mo. —BS, University of Missouri, 1950; MA. University of Missouri, 1952. Exhibitions: *Joslyn Biennial*, Omaha, Neb.; *Mid-America Art Biennial*, Owensboro, Ky.; *Mid-Four,* Nelson-Atkins Museum, Kansas City, Mo. Represented in Collections: Continental Insurance Corp., N.Y., N.Y.; Hallmark Collection, Kansas City, Mo.; Sheldon Memorial Art Gallery, Lincoln, Neb.

NORMAN GEE — Page 28
Born 1940, San Francisco, Calif. —BFA, California College of Arts and Crafts, 1965; MFA, California College of Arts and Crafts, 1967. Exhibitions: *Work by Norman Gee,* Wichita Art Museum; *Invitational,* Wing Luke Memorial Museum, Seattle, Wash.; John B. Davis Gallery, Idaho State University, Nocotelle, Idaho. Represented in Collections: Murray State University, Murray, Ky.; Wing Luke Memorial Museum, Seattle, Wash.; Mulvane Art Center, Topeka, Kan.

RICHARD GILLESPIE — Page 30
Born 1935, Kansas City, Kan. —BFA, Kansas City Art Institute, Mo. 1965; MA, Stanford University, Calif. 1968. Exhibitions: *The Society of the Four Arts 1974 Competition,* Palm Beach, Fla.; *National Invitational Sculpture Competition,* Akstom Foundation; *Two Man Invitational*, University of South Dakota; *Dreams and Dislocations-Visionary Images*, Douglas Drake Gallery, Kansas City, Mo. Represented in Collections: Mr. & Mrs. John M. Dodig, Hollywood, Calif; Dr. & Mrs. R. Nadeau, Kansas City, Mo.; Dr. & Mrs. Horquitz, San Francisco, Calif.

THOMAS P. GORMALLY — Page 32
Born 1949, Minneapolis, Minn. —BFA, Minneapolis College of Art and Design, Minn. 1977; MFA, Wichita State University, Kan. 1979. Exhibitions: *Tom Gormally; A Selection of Sculpture & Paintings,* Blanden Art Museum, Ft. Dodge, Iowa; *Selections from the New York Chemical Bank Collection,* N.Y., N.Y.; *A Kansas Collection,* National Museum of Women in the Arts., Washington, D.C.

MARILYN GRISHAM — Page 24
Born 1940, El Dorado, Kan. —BFA, Ottawa University, Ottawa, Kan. Exhibitions: *Woven Works: Tradition and Innovation Invitational,* University of Wisconsin, Green Bay, Wis.; *For The Floor,* American Craft Museum, N.Y., N.Y.; *Fiber Exhibition & Small Expressions*, Handweavers Guild of America, Toronto, Canada. Represented in Collections: Chicago Board of Trade, Chicago, Ill.; The Hands On Gallery, Wichita Art Museum, Wichita, Kan.; Continental Insurance Co., Dallas, Texas

LYNN HAVEL — Page 34
Born 1946, Clyde, Kan. —MFA, Wichita State University, Kan. 1976; MA, Fort Hays State University, Kan. 1970. Exhibitions: *38th Salon de la Jeune Peinture,* Grand Palais, Paris, France; *ART Made in USA: Positionen Junger Kunst*, Deutsch-Ameridanisches Institute, Regensburg, West Germany; *Works by Lynn Havel,* 2nd Street Gallery, Charlottesville, Va. Represented in Collections: College of Architecture, Clemson University, S.C.; Transco Energy Company, Houston, Texas; McDonald's, Oak Brook, Ill.

JON HAVENER — Page 36
Born 1950, Jacksonville, Fla. —BFA, Cleveland Institute of Art, Ohio 1973; MFA, Cranbrook Academy of Art, Mich. 1975. Exhibitions: *Form Beyond Function*, Mitchell Museum of Art, Mt. Vernon, Ill.; *Last National Sculpture Exhibition*, University of Georgia, Athens, Ga.; *National Jewelry/Small Sculpture Invitational*, University of Arizona, Tempe, Ariz. Represented in Collections: United States Comptroller of Currency, Omaha, Nebr./Kansas City, Mo.; University of Kansas, Dept. of Engineering, Lawrence, Kan.

NICHOLAS HILL — Page 38
Born 1952, Sault Ste. Marie, Mich. —BFA, Michigan State University, 1974; MA, University of Iowa, 1976; MFS University of Iowa, 1977. Exhibitions: *Rutgers National Works on Paper*, Rutgers University, Camden, N.J.; Woodstock National Painting Exhibition, Woodstock, N.Y.; *Somertown Gallery lst International Biennial Print Exhibition*, Somers, N.Y. Represented in Collections: Nelson-Atkins Museum of Art, Kansas City, Mo.; University of Iowa, Iowa City, Iowa; Prince Mohammed Bukiah, Brunei, Borneo

JAMES HOLMES — Page 40
Born 1950, Wichita, Kan. —BFA, University of Kansas, 1973; MFA, School of Art, Institute of Chicago, 1978. Exhibitions: *Work by James Holmes*, Paris Gibson Square Center for the Arts, Great Falls, Mont.; *20th Joslyn Biennial*, Omaha, Neb.; *Works by James Holmes*, Pasadena City College, Calif. Represented in Collections: Best Products, Richmond, Va.; Prudential Insurance, Newark, N.J.; Shook, Hardy & Bacon Law Firm, Kansas City, Mo.

MICHAEL FLORIAN JILG —Page 42
Born 1947, Great Bend, Kan. —MA, Fort Hays State University, Kan 1970; MFA Wichita State University, Kan. 1972. Exhibitions: *lst Annual Kansas Artists Competition*, Judicial Bldg., Topeka, Kan.; *Kansas Watercolor Tri-State Competition*, Wichita Art Museum, Wichita, Kan.; *International Miniature Print Traveling Exhibit;* Pratt Graphics, N.Y., N.Y. Represented in collections: Joslyn Art Museum, Omaha, Neb.; Santa Reparata Graphics Institute, Florence, Italy; Purdue University Galleries, Purdue, Ind.

CIMA KATZ — Page 44
Born 1949, New York, N.Y. —BFA, Carnegie-Mellon University, Pa. 1971; MFA, Indiana University, 1974. Exhibitions: *Colorprint, USA*, Lubbock, Texas; *Mid-Four*, Nelson-Atkins Museum, Kansas City, Mo.; *Premio Internazionale Biella per L'Incisione*, Biella, Italy. Represented in Collections: United States Information Agency; J. B. Speed Museum, Louisville, Ky.; Spencer Museum of Art, Lawrence, Kan.

DAN KIRCHHEFER — Page 46
Born 1947, Hastings, Neb. —BFA, University of Nebraska, 1971; MFS, University of Kansas, 1985. Exhibitions: *6th Annual National Small Works Show*, N.Y., N.Y.; *American Drawings IV*, Portsmouth, Va.; *Mid-Four*, Nelson-Atkins Museum, Kansas City, Mo. Represented in Collections: Portsmouth Community Art Center and Museums, Portsmouth, Va; Edinboro University of Pennsylvania, Edinboro, Pa.; Kansas State University, Dept. of Art/University Collections, Manhattan, Kan.

SILVIA KOLYER — Page 48
Born 1941, East Germany; Died 1986, Wichita, Kan. —BFA, Herron School of Art, Indiana University, 1982; MFA,Wichita State University, Kan. 1986. Exhibitions: *Kansas Six*, Mulvane Gallery, Topeka, Kan.; *Prairie Art Exhibition*, Sterling, Kan.; *The13th Michiana Regional*, South Bend, Ind. Represented in Collections: Wayne Vincent, Secretary, Indiana Arts Commission; Della Pachelo, Editor, *Arts Insight;* David & Theresa Ehrlich, Indianapolis, Ind.

MARGO KREN — Page 50
Born 1939, Houston, Texas —BS, University of Wisconsin, 1966; MFA, University of Iowa, 1979. Exhibitions: *Narrative/Personal Visions 1985*, Downey Museum of Art, Los Angeles, Calif.; *Directions: Personal Iconography 1986*, Spiva Art Center, Joplin Mo.; *Tenth Annual National Invitiational Drawing Exhibition*, Emporia State University, Emporia, Kan. Represented in Collections: Mutual Benefit Life Insurance Co., Kansas City, Mo.; El Paso Museum of Art, El Paso, Texas; Western Michigan University, Kalamazoo, Mich.

KATHLEEN KUCHAR — Page 52
Born 1942, Meadow Grove, Neb. —MS, Fort Hays State University, Kan. 1966; MFA, Wichita State University, Kan. 1974. Exhibitions: *Watercolor USA*, Springfield Art Museum, Springfield, Mo.; *65th Annual National Watercolor Society Exhibition*, Brea, Calif; *Rocky Mountain National Watermedia Exhibition*, Golden, Colo. Represented in Collections: Crescent Cardboard Co.; Nebraska Arts Collection; Wichita State University, Wichita, Kan.

MARGIE KUHN — Page 54
Born 1952, Kansas City, Kan. —BGS, University of Kansas, 1975. Exhibitions: *American Watercolor Society Annual*, N.Y., N.Y.; *Watercolor USA* , Springfield, Mo.; *Mid-Four*, Nelson-Atkins Museum, Kansas City, Mo. Represented in Collections: Interex Research Corp. Lawrence, Kan., Borg-Warner Acceptance Corp., Kansas City, Mo.; Gage & Tucker, Overland Park, Kan.

RANDALL J. KUST — Page 56
Born 1948, Green Bay, Wis. —BFA, Midwestern State University, Texas 1975; MFA, Wichita State University, Kan. 1979. Exhibitions: *Winners, Traveling Exhibition of M-AAA/NEA Fellowship Award Winners in Printmaking, Drawing, Artist Books and Photography*; Washington, D.C.; *New American Graphics 2*, Touring Exhibition of Contemporary Prints, University of Wisconsin and Madison Art Center; *Wesleyan 2nd International Traveling Exhibition of Prints and Drawings*, Wesleyan College, Macon, Ga. Represented in Collections: American Embassy in Tel Aviv, Israel; The Boston Printmakers, Lexington, Mass.; Las Vegas Art Museum, Las Vegas, Nev.

ELIZABETH LAYTON — Page 58
Born 1909, Wellsville, Kan. —Two drawing courses, Ottawa University, Kan. 1977. Exhibitions: *National Council on Aging*; Washington, D.C.: *Works of Elizabeth Layton*, Phoenix Art Museum, Phoenix, Ariz.; *Works of Elizabeth Layton*, Chicago Public Library Cultural, Chicago, Ill. Represented in Collections: Permanent Collection, Wichita Art Museum; Wichita, Kan.; National Museum of Women in the Arts, Washington, D.C.; Mulvane Art Museum, Topeka, Kan.

JUDY BURNS MC CREA — Page 60
Born 1944, Wichita, Kan. —BFA, Wichita State University, Kan. 1967; MFA, Wichita State University, Kan. 1970. Exhibitions: *National Drawing Competition*, Berkeley Gallery, Meriden, N.H.; *Winners, Mid-America Biennial 1989 of Mid-America Arts Alliance/NEA Fellowship Award Winners.* Represented in Collections: Hallmark Corp., Kansas City, Mo.; Minot State College, Minot, N.D.; Wichita State University, Wichita, Kan.

NANCY K. MEANS — Page 62
Born 1943, Wichita, Kan. —BFA, Wichita State University, Kan. 1975; MFA, Wichita State University, Kan. 1977. Exhibitions: *Arizona National Annual Competition*, Scottsdale Center for the Arts, Scottsdale, Ariz.; *Marietta National*, Grover M. Hermann Fine Arts Center, Marietta, Ohio; *Fourth Biennial Faculty Exhibition*, Edwin A. Uhlrich Museum of Art, Wichita, Kan. Represented in Collections: Association for Community Arts Councils of Kansas; Wichita State University, Wichita, Kan., Dr. & Mrs. Frank Brosius, Wichita, Kan.

JIM MUNCE — Page 64
Born 1938, Sioux Falls, S.D. —BFA, Minneapolis School of Art, Minn. 1966; MFA, Indiana University, 1971. Exhibitions: *Invitational Intaglio Exhibition*, University of Louisville, Ky.; *Boston Printmakers 38th National Print Exhibition*, DeCorduva Museum, Lincoln, Mass.; *National Drawing Exhibition*, Trenton State College, Trenton, N. J. Represented in Collections: Brooklyn Museum, New York, N.Y.; Palace of the Legion of Honor, San Francisco, Calif.; Mitsubishi Corp., Tokyo, Japan

JOHN NEWMAN — Page 66
Born 1948, Roar, Ark. —BFA, Columbus College of Art & Design, Ohio, 1970; MFA, University of Kansas, 1982. Exhibitions: *UCLA National Student Print Exhibition*, Calif; *Mid-Four*, Nelson-Atkins Museum of Art, Kansas City, Mo.; *The Neighborhood*, Rockhurst College, Kansas City, Mo. Represented in Collections: Spencer Art Museum, Lawrence, Kan.; Des Moines Art Center, Des Moines, Iowa; Richard Hollander, Kansas City, Mo.

DIANE NEWTON — Page 68
Born 1947, Omaha, Neb. —BFA, University of Nebraska, 1969; MFA, Wichita State University, Kan. 1980. Exhibitions: *Six from Kansas*, Miller Gallery, Cincinnatti, Ohio; *Rutgers National Works on Paper*, Rutgers University, Camden, N.J.; *Kansas Six*, Mulvane Art Center, Topeka, Kan. Represented in Collections: Fahad Al-Athel, Riyadh, Saudi Arabia; Rent-A-Center, Corp. Headquarters, Wichita, Kan.; Adams & McCarthy, Wichita, Kan.

FRANK NICHOLS — Page 70
Born 1935, Arkansas City, Kan. —BSE, Emporia State, Kan.; MFA, Wichita State University, Kan. Exhibitions: *North Dakota Annual Printmaking and Drawing*, Grandforks, N.D.; *Fourth Annual Paper in Particular*, Columbia, Mo.; *Carrier Foundation Competition*, Belle Meade, N.J. Represented in Collections: Wichita State University, Wichita, Kan.; Chaffin, Inc., Dodge City, Kan.; Mulvane Art Center, Topeka, Kan.

BEA OPELKA — Page 72
Born 1937, Kaunas, Lithuania —BS, University of Illinois, 1959. Exhibitions: *Pen Women's Bi-Annual Midwest Competition*, St. Louis, Mo.; *The Kansas Landscape*, Traveling Exhibition sponsored by Kansas Arts Commission; *A Kansas Collection*, National Museum of Women in the Arts, Washington, D.C. Represented in Collections: Kansas University Medical School, Wichita, Kan.; Kansas University Alumn Assn., Lawrence, Kan.; Art Planning Consultants, N.Y.

MICHAEL OTT — Page 74
Born 1945, Bartlesville, Okla. —BFA, University of Colorado, 1967; MA, University of California, 1969. Exhibitions: *Visual Fun, Number One, National Humor in Art*, Traveling Exhibition curated by Walter Askin; *The Creative Process: 10 years at Ragdale*, Traveling Exhibition curated by Evadene Judge; *Realist Watercolors*, Alpha Gallery, Denver, Colo. Represented in Collections: Hallmark Collection, Kansas City, Mo.; D.S.T. Computer Collection

MARY F. PALFFY — Page 76
Born 1954, Vienna, Austria —BA, Montana State University, 1979; MFA in Printmaking, Northwestern University, Ill. 1984; MFA in Painting, Northwestern University, Ill. 1984. Exhibitions: *Traditions and Alternatives*, Brainerd Art Gallery, Potsdam, N.Y.; *Springfield Art League 65th National Exhibition*, The George Walter Vincent Smith Art Museum, Springfield, Mass.; *U.S. National Fine Arts Competition and International Exhibition*, State Capitol Building, Tallahassee, Fla. Represented in Collections: AT&T, Chicago, Ill.

DEBORAH SCHLIER — Page 78
Born 1957, Amarillo, Texas —BFA, Wichita State University, Kan. 1981; MFA, Wichita State University, 1988. Exhibitions: *25th National Print Competition*, Brainard Art Gallery, Potsdam, N.Y.; *18th National Works on Paper*, Dulin Art Gallery, Knoxville, Tenn.; *18th Annual Spiva Exhibition*, Spiva Art Center, Joplin, Mo. Represented in Collections: Beech Aircraft Corporation, Wichita, Kan.; Potsdam College, Potsdam, N.Y.

KATHLEEN SHANAHAN — Page 80
Born 1947, Galesburg, Ill. —BFA, University of Michigan, 1969; MFA, University of Arizona, 1974. Exhibitions: *KWS Tri-State Watercolor Exhibition*, Wichita Art Museum, Wichita, Ks.; *Mid-Four*, Nelson-Atkins Museum, Kansas City, Mo.; *Works on Paper*, Spokane, Wash. Represented in Collections: Wichita Art Museum, Wichita, Ks; *Maison et Jardin Magazine*, Paris, France; Tatsuro Nikata Curator of National Museum of Art, Osaka, Japan

GORDON SHERMAN — Page 82
Born 1951, Hastings, Neb. —B.A, Fort Hays State University, Kan. 1973; MFA, Wichita State University, Kan. 1976. Exhibitions: *Drawings U.S.A.*, Minnesota Museum of Art, St. Paul, Minn.; *11th Dulin National Print and Drawing Competition*, Knoxville, Tenn.; *2nd Biennial Faculty Exhibition*, Ulrich Museum of Art, Wichita, Kan. Represented in Collections: Tulsa Public Library, Tulsa, Okla.; Patrick Treu, Victoria, Australia; Mr. & Mrs. M. Wilcox, Greeley, Colo.

ROGER SHIMOMURA — Page 84
Born 1939, Seattle, Wash. —BA, University of Washington, 1961; MFA, Syracuse University, N.Y., 1969. Exhibitions: *Works by Roger Shimomura*, Gallery Heian, Kyoto, Japan; *Works by Roger Shimomura*, Frannell Gallery, Tokyo, Japan; *Current Painting in America*, Indianapolis Art Museum, Indianapolis, Ind. Represented in Collections: Seattle Art Museum, Seattle, Wash.; Denver Art Museum, Denver, Colo.; Birmingham Art Museum, Birmingham, Ala.

RICHARD T. SIEGMAN — Page 86
Born 1949, Cincinnati, Ohio —BFA, Northern Kentucky State University, 1975; MFA, Wichita State University, Kan. 1980. Exhibitions: *Rutgers National Drawing Competition*, Rutgers University, Camden, N.J.; *280 Exhibition*, Huntington Art Museum, Huntington, W.Va.; *Works on Paper, 2nd Annual Invitational*, Wichita, Kan. Represented in Collections: Northern Kentucky State University, Highland Heights, Ky.; Wichita State University, Wichita, Kan.; Sr. Services, Inc., Wichita, Kan.

ROBERT SUDLOW — Page 88
Born 1920, Holton, Kan. —BFA, University of Kansas, 1942; MFA, California College of Arts and Crafts, 1955. Exhibitions: *Summer Invitational*, Nelson-Atkins Art Museum, Kansas City, Mo.; *Kansas Landscape Traveling Exhibition*, Kansas Arts Commission; *A Sense of Place, The Artist and the American Land*, National Traveling Exhibition. Represented in Collections: Yellow Freight, Kansas City, Mo.; Mulvane Art Center, Washburn University, Topeka, Kan.; Mr. David Wittig, N.Y., N.Y.

JACK WILSON — Page 90
Born 1953, Wichita, Kan. —BFA, Wichita State University, Kan. 1978; MFA, Printmaking, Wichita State University, Kan. 1985. Exhibitions: *11th Color Print, U.S.A.*, Texas Tech University, Lubbock, Texas; *Dreamstates*, Artists Registry, Inc., Hilton Inn East, Wichita, Ks.; *18th National Works on Paper*, Dulin Gallery, Knoxville, Tenn. Represented in Collections: Dulin Gallery of Art, Knoxville, Tenn.; Carol Belove, Petaluma, Calif.; Jason Pollen, Kansas City, Mo.

RANAL YOUNG — Page 92
Born 1951, Nashville, Tenn. —BA, Midwestern State University, Texas, 1973; MFA, Wichita State University, Kan. 1975. Exhibitions: *72nd American Annual*, Newport Art Assn., Newport, R.I.; *Galex 17*, Galesburg Civic Art Center, Galesburg, Ill.; *Mr. Godey's Ladies Revisited*, Wichita Art Museum, Wichita, Kan. Represented in Collections: Mid-Kansas Federal Savings & Loan Assn., Wichita, Kan.; Stephan Advertising Agency, Wichita, Kan.; Ginger Tarrer, Wichita, Kan.

artists registry, inc.
p.o. box 8833
wichita, kansas 67208